LEXINGTON, VIRGINIA:
History Lessons
from a
Country Church

LEXINGTON, VIRGINIA:

History Lessons
from a
Country Church

VOLUME I

Dr. Horace Douty

1 3 5 7 9 10 8 6 4 2

Library of Congress Control Number: 2014956466

Lexington, Virginia:
History Lessons from a Country Church
Volume I
Dr. Horace Douty

p. cm.
1. History: Virginia
2. Religion: Presbyterian
3. History: General

I. Douty, Horace, 1932— II. Title.

ISBN 13: 978-0-9909653-0-5 (hardcover : alk. paper)

Cover Design by Charles Lovelace • Book Design by Emilie Davis

Mariner Media, Inc.
131 West 21st Street
Buena Vista, VA 24416
Tel: 540-264-0021
www.marinermedia.com

Printed in the United States of America

This book is printed on acid-free paper meeting the
requirements of the American Standard for Permanence of Paper
for Printed Library Materials.

Table of Contents

Acknowledgments

Writing a book is one thing. Publishing it is another quite different undertaking. I am fortunate to know people who can make things happen in territory totally unfamiliar to me. Dr. Clinton Anderson, himself an author, knew how many steps are involved in publishing. First he encouraged me to write these stories. Then he spent countless hours providing information, rounding up a team, selecting photos, writing captions, and getting bids.

My daughter Ellen Moore volunteered impressive skills that surprised me. Somewhere she has acquired technical experience enabling her to transmit electronically every kind of data needed for this book. She quickly became project manager, captain of the team, and editor. Her husband Harrison is a professional videographer and photographer. They have driven several times from their home in Fairfax into Rockbridge, taking pictures and helping me understand the complexities of our new computer world. I have to agree with Clinton when he says, "Without your daughter, this book would not be published."

Bruce MacDonald is another miracle worker. Occupied as a professor at Washington and Lee University, he yet made time to draw all the illustrations, design the dust jacket, and give consistent encouragement and advice. Bruce also understands current technology. I had thought publishers required typed pages. He knew all that was obsolete, completely replaced by compact discs and digital files. I thank Bruce for bringing me into the twenty-first century.

Evelyn Ayers quietly moved mostly behind the scenes, producing old photos, keeping accurate records, and speaking words of encouragement. Her extensive organizational and creative capabilities came as a surprise to me.

John William Johnston proved to be a gold mine of information. Although he has spent much of his life outside Rockbridge, he grew up on South Buffalo, the home of his illustrious ancestors. John shared written and oral tradition, some of which is now preserved in this publication. John's sister Mary Brady was also generous in providing material regarding the Diehls of Dundee. Mrs. George Diehl (Iva Shafer) was another native of South Buffalo, and the aunt of John and Mary.

Dr. James Parsons gave me much of the story of Rapp's Mill. He and his wife live in the ancestral home of Matthias Rapp, inventor of the turbine that powered his unique mill. The home is also unusual, with interior walls made of tightly stacked two by fours. Dr. Parsons is another native who moved back to Buffalo, after a distinguished career as a chemist in New England.

I am indebted to Lisa McCown, keeper of Special Collections in the Leyburn Library of Washington and Lee University. Regardless of the subject, Lisa knew how to produce documentation every time I asked. It was pleasant to discover that Lisa has family roots strongly connected to Oxford Church.

Jean Tardy Clark, director of tourism for Rockbridge, knows virtually every person in the area. She was able to direct me to unexpected sources of information. She knows which territory is friendly and how I should handle those situations that are not. Jean has served as a remarkably able clerk of Oxford session for a number of years. Working beside her in the church has been an honor and a pleasure for me even when the pace is breathless and demanding. Jean's heritage in Rockbridge runs deep, long, and wide.

Herbert and Mary Frances Rhodenizer are two more pillars in Oxford. Both are products of Buffalo and its legacy, eager to share their wisdom, skills and friendship. Herb is the expert in charge of the ancient graveyard and is able to remember every detail. Mary Frances gave me helpful notes regarding her family, the Halls, who for more than two centuries have helped shape the stories of Rockbridge. Other church members also gave me useful material, notably John and Betty Ayers and Mildred and E.G. Huffman.

I spent memorable hours with Bill Leech in the stone house below Oxford Church. I listened carefully as he guided me through local history. Although his death in 2008 was an abrupt loss for me, I am grateful for the affection and the wisdom he gave so generously. The chapter which bears his name in this book is the only one I did not write. My thanks go to his grandchildren Jacob and Holly for loving him and for remembering and writing. Leech leadership has abounded on Buffalo from the beginning. Charlie and Linda, along with Will and Sharon, keep that tradition alive and glowing in this century. A separate book would be required to record the Leech family story, which certainly merits preservation. Beau and Jennifer, you are young, intelligent, and live here. Start writing.

I thank Margaret Wallin, current owner of the Woodside Church building, for firsthand information about the inspiring activity at Union Run and how it has connections with Oxford.

Charlie and Steve Potter and their families own much of the land bordering Oxford. They cheerfully guided me across Meeting House Lane, that old path so filled with fading memories. From Meeting House Lane on Potter property came the wonderful photo that gives the reader a perspective of Oxford seen long ago by the Collierstown residents. For ninety years they walked across the hills and descended to the mother church on Sabbath mornings.

Before I finally mastered the mysteries of Microsoft Word, I wrote my manuscripts by hand. Kitty Falls and Patricia Donald volunteered significant help as they deciphered and typed those first lessons. I owe them hearty thanks.

Jeremy Leadbetter of Andre Studios has been consistently ready to reproduce and scan many photographs for publication. The staff at Rockbridge Regional Library came to my aid at every request. Nancy Sorrells, another student of church history, served as a competent proofer. Charles Lovelace deserves special thanks for his careful work of formatting this entire book.

I thank the homeowners who permitted me to photograph and publish material that is connected with the stories from Oxford. I am grateful for the careful writings of Dr. George Diehl, pastor of Oxford for nearly twenty years; he became a recognized authority on genealogy and Rockbridge history. I have absorbed information from Morton's *History of Rockbridge County*, Foote's *Sketches of Virginia*, and *Proceedings of the Rockbridge Historical Society*. The published annals of local churches provided a wealth of knowledge.

It is my good fortune to live in a place where heroes past and present are found in uncommon abundance. They give me something to write about. In addition I have a congregation showing up each week eager to hear a story, which gives me a reason to write. When I look out there and see more than a hundred eyeballs turned expectantly toward me, I find it compelling.

My wife Ellen deserves enormous appreciation. She was the first to suggest these lessons be bound into a book. As I read each rough draft aloud, she offered improvements for nearly every chapter. At no time did she deviate from her conviction that the time-consuming project was worth completing. I thank Ellen earnestly for such unflinching support, steadying me under all conditions.

Chronology of Oxford Church in Rockbridge, Virginia

1740 Settlers penetrate the western frontier of Virginia and build homesteads in the Great Valley, including the Buffalo Creek watershed.

1750 A "Presbyterian Society" forms at Whistle Creek and begins meeting at "Hall's Meeting House." Residents in Upper Buffalo walk two hours each way to attend. Reverend Alexander Craighead is an occasional preacher there. The name is changed to "Monmouth" after the Revolutionary War.

1758 A Presbyterian Society begins to meet at the log fort where Oxford Church stands today.

1772 The name "Oxford Meeting House" first appears. Meeting House Lane brings settlers from Collierstown to Oxford. They begin the practice of burying their dead in the churchyard out front. Each early pastor is required to serve several churches in a large geographical area.

1777 Captain James Hall and his Buffalo militia are involved in the execution of the powerful Shawnee chief Cornstalk who had led deadly raids against frontier settlements. Captain Hall builds and operates "Hall's School" near the church, on the Hall family's land adjoining Oxford.

1788 Reverend William Graham, the brilliant founder of what would become Washington and Lee University, serves as pastor of Oxford, Monmouth, Timber Ridge and Lexington.

1795   Reverend Samuel Houston becomes pastor of Oxford, Falling Spring and High Bridge churches. His first wife is Mary Hall, sister of Captain James Hall. Houston builds a home and school at Rural Valley, directly across Short Hill Mountain from Oxford.

1800–1814 Reverend Daniel Blain, professor at Washington College, becomes pastor at Oxford. The log fort is replaced by a stone church in 1811. Blain dies suddenly in 1814, the only Oxford pastor to die in office.

1816   Reverend Andrew Davidson moves to the Oxford Community, serving as an exceptionally fruitful pastor until the early 1830s when he begins focusing most of his attention on the Ship Rock Meeting House at Collierstown where the new highway crossed North Mountain. The road is called the Lexington-Covington Turnpike.

1841   The Oxford stone church is closed. Reverend Davidson moves all activity and communion ware to "New Oxford" at busy Collierstown, using the Ship Rock site. Oxford Cemetery, the only public burying ground on Buffalo, remains active. The dead are transported across Meeting House Lane for burial.

1844   Presbytery organizes a new church at the graveyard with the stone church. The new church is officially named "Old Oxford."

1856   A brick church is constructed at the west end of Meeting House Lane. The name changes from Ship Rock to New Oxford and finally to Collierstown Presbyterian Church.

1866   The Civil War has ended. Reverend John Scott, a confederate chaplain, becomes Oxford's pastor, attracting many ex-soldiers to the church. Construction of a new brick church begins in 1868 with the strong involvement of Confederate veterans.

1869   The brick church is completed, with a partial basement, even though Reverend Scott has moved to another field. Dr. J.L. Kilpatrick from the faculty of Washington and Lee University fills the pulpit regularly. When General Lee dies, Dr. Kilpatrick acts as college president during some stressful years.

1869–1894 During this quarter-century Oxford is without regular services for half the time. A Jewish merchant named Henry Heilbroner presents Oxford Church with a handsome pulpit bible in honor of his comrade-in-arms Granville Campbell.

1894   The tide turns. Reverend William Bailey moves to Bolivar, later called Murat, which is midway between his two churches, Oxford and Woodside. For the first time Oxford builds a manse for the exclusive use of her pastors. It is located a mile upstream from the brick church.

1902   Reverend Thomas Mowbray moves into the new manse and becomes Oxford's pastor. Under his leadership Palmer Academy is built, the first rural high school in the county. Mowbray proves to be a popular pastor, but when he is arrested for disregarding the quarantine order he feels he must relocate. Sidney Saville, a gifted Oxford elder, keeps the school going after Reverend Mowbray moves away.

1910   A bell tower is added to the brick church.

1915   Mr. and Mrs. S.A. McHenry donate their farm bell for installation in the bell tower.

1916   A hole is cut in the sanctuary floor so that an indoor stairway can be built for access to the basement. Oxford provides outreach ministry with chapels and Sunday schools at Rapps Mill, Hamilton School, Oakdale and Bolivar Mill.

1949   Dr. George W. Diehl arrives from Texas to serve Oxford for eighteen fruitful years.

1952   The Murat Women's Club renovates the overgrown church cemetery.

1962   The Educational Building is constructed.

1967   A new brick manse is built beside the church and the old manse is sold.

2008   Oxford celebrates her 250th anniversary on September 14. A state historical marker is installed at the intersection of Oxford Lane and Blue Grass Trail noting the church as an official historic landmark. A monument with bronze plaque memorializing Captain James Hall is placed near the entrance to the church.

Since Dr. Diehl retired in 1968, Oxford has enjoyed a virtually unbroken line of ministers to the present year 2008. That fact alone represents a change in the church's 250-year history. Oxford has survived without a pastor for a total of 60 years. Supply preachers filled the pulpit for another 61 years, which means that the church has had resident pastors slightly more than half the time, about 130 of the 250 years.

For a complete listing of Oxford pastors see Diehl, *Old Oxford And Her Families*. The following ministers have served since that list was made in 1968:

1968 to 1978   James Guthrie

1979 to 1997   Barton Hellmuth

1999 to 2006   Robert Whitehouse

2006 to Present   Horace Douty

Author's Preface

When I began my ministry to Oxford Church in 2006, little did I know that a book would come from it. I was first impressed by the setting of unsurpassed natural beauty. There sat the church on a green knoll, surrounded by mountain and meadow. Buffalo Creek meandered below, the sparkling trout stream that gave the area its name. Oxford Valley, fertile and uncluttered, drew my eyes southward. As I stood at the church's front door, the sweeping vista before me was breathtaking, a photographer's delight.

My second impression was of history. A church that has lived for more than a quarter-millennium surely must have a noble heritage. I was motivated to seek out some of the stories. I shared them with the congregation, assuming that most of the material was familiar to them. Each Sunday morning I presented a three-minute history lesson as part of the worship service. Two things surprised me: (1) the people were eager for Rockbridge history, and (2) most of them were unaware of their uncommon heritage. As requests came regularly for copies of the lessons it became clear that they should be preserved. The idea of a book was hatched.

The reader will quickly notice that this is not a history book. It is rather a collection of stories about our Rockbridge ancestors. Many of the anecdotes have a direct connection with Oxford. Others reach beyond Buffalo to embrace the county. My aim is to spark an interest in each subject as a springboard for further study. The book may serve as a quick and compact reference for Rockbridge's rich history. My most difficult challenge was to keep the lessons short and interesting. No doubt scholarly historians will wince at my omissions and inaccuracies, which I hope are few.

Oxford Church set September 14, 2008, as the date for celebrating her 250th anniversary. That date struck me as a logical deadline for the publication of this book. It is obvious to me that many other stories remain to be recounted. Perhaps a second and even third book can be the outcome.

As I uncovered stories about the amazing accomplishments of Rockbridge heroes, questions formed in my mind, questions that do not go away. How can it be that we don't even know where the Lady Magdalena was laid to rest? Famous for her strength and beauty, she deserves to be spoken of as "the Mother of Rockbridge." We talk about Cyrus McCormick, but why do we hear so little about his neighbor, the venerable Archibald Alexander?

Almost everyone knows how General Robert E. Lee helped keep the Lexington college alive after the Civil War. He is venerated and remembered, as he should be. Yet just outside Lee's tomb lies William Graham, founder of the college. Why do we hear so little about him? Margaret Junkin Preston won fame as Lexington's poet laureate of the south. Are her poignant rhymes being read to children today?

I believe it is well for us to remember and revere the remarkable souls. They are part of Rockbridge. They helped shape us who live here. We are cradled in their glowing legacy. Our pride is quickened and our souls are strengthened when we speak of them.

It is my hope that this small collection will encourage others, wherever they live, to remember and recount their own heritage. Our nation hungers for heroes. Our children instinctively know that the procession of celebrities offered by the entertainment industry usually prove to be imperfect role models. Why not bring time-tested legends out of the archives? We can make them come alive again. We are blessed with an endless reserve of gifted leaders. Their examples shine and beckon and encourage. Their spirits hover about us.

Let the creative soul of Reverend Samuel Houston be our model. Let the courage of little Mary Moore inspire us. Let John Robinson show how an illiterate weaver can achieve enormous success, and let his subsequent generosity quicken our compassion. These astonishing people lifted up their eyes unto the same hills we see.

They breathed the same Rockbridge air as we. They drank from the waters that refresh us today. When we allow them to nourish our souls, they will.

> *And when the fight is fierce, the warfare long,*
> *Steals on the ear the distant triumph song*
> *And hearts are brave again, and arms are strong.*
>   *Alleluia!*
>
>   — W.W. How,
>   *For All The Saints,*
>   *Who From Their Labors Rest*, 1864

Lesson 1:
Rockbridge Beginnings

O ur part of the Rockbridge story in Virginia begins with the year 1737. Ephraim McDowell and his family had set up a camp near the place we now call Raphine. They had journeyed to America a few years earlier and had gradually made their way from Philadelphia into Virginia's great valley, searching for fertile, affordable land. Ephraim was getting old, but he had some strong people with him. His feisty daughter Mary was there with her husband James Greenlee. Ephraim's son John, who had married Magdalena Woods, the famous frontier beauty, was in the camp with his wife and their small son James. The group may have contained as many as a dozen Scot-Irish folk, including servants and other family members.

The countryside was wild but promising, and the family had some knowledge of the area. In 1716 Governor Alexander Spotswood and his "Knights Of The Golden Horseshoe" had crossed the Blue Ridge and explored part of the valley well north of the McDowell campsite. A number of brave families already lived near present-day Staunton. All of the settlers were somewhat apprehensive, because ancient treaties had once recognized the crest of the Blue Ridge as the official boundary line for Indian territory.

As a venison dinner was being prepared one evening, a man named Benjamin Borden walked into the camp with some astonishing news. He announced that the governor of Virginia had given him 100,000 acres of this new land. There were two provisions: he had to locate the tract and he must persuade people to live on it. John McDowell, a skilled surveyor, immediately offered to determine the boundaries of Borden's grant. Furthermore, the entire family was willing to make it their home. A delighted Borden struck a deal right there by the campfire, and the McDowells became the first landowners in the Borden Grant.

One thousand acres was theirs for the choosing. Rockbridge settlement had begun.

You may be wondering what prompted Virginia's English governor to be so generous with Benjamin Borden. There are some who claim that Borden had delivered a live buffalo calf to Williamsburg, pleasing the governor with the unusual gift. Mary McDowell Greenlee, famed for her sharp tongue, snorted that Borden had won some sort of wager during the hilarity of a drinking party at the governor's mansion. Mary never cared for the Bordens and was less than elated when a few years later Ben Borden Jr. became her brother-in-law through his marriage to the widow Magdalena. The truth is that the governor was encouraging Scot-Irish and German speaking dissenters to settle in the valley and serve as a buffer between established English settlements east of the Blue Ridge and the French and Indians in the Ohio River Valley.

In the vastness of Virginia's "back parts," that fortuitous meeting between Borden and McDowell seems miraculous. There are, however, some rational explanations. Both parties were on the "Great Path" through the Valley of Virginia, a trail that had existed hundreds of years as the north-south course for buffalo herds and Native Americans. Because of settlement pressures from the East and fur trading pressures from the West, Native Americans had not inhabited the Valley for several decades, though they had cleared much of the land by annual burning. The Indians cultivated the northern part of the valley for growing maize, or corn, and they kept the southern half in open grassland for the benefit of grazing buffalo. It was considered something of a game preserve for native hunting parties. When Borden encountered the McDowells, he knew he was very near the edge of his grant. He could tell by the flow of running water. At this very point in the Great Valley, the waters divide. Face north, and all streams can be seen running northward into the Shenandoah that meets the Potomac at Harpers Ferry. Turn around, and the waters drain southward into the James. Although the settlers could not have known it at the time, they were standing on topography that in forty years was near the northern county line of Rockbridge, Virginia.

Today, most people are surprised to learn that the Raphine area has elevations of more than two thousand feet. Fifteen miles to the east, at the crest of Afton Mountain, the U.S Geological Survey has placed a marker on U.S. Rt. 250 that reads "elevation 1985 feet." This means that the center of the valley is higher than the crest of the Blue Ridge, in the gap now used by two major highways, including Interstate 64. John McDowell knew it, and he camped at that high point of the Great Valley, where the waters divide.

After the contract with Borden, the jubilant McDowells selected their one thousand acres some ten miles southward on the Great Path. Around them lay fresh and fertile pasture lands, ready for cultivation. An unburned length of virgin forest stood before them, from which they harvested logs for their sturdy home. They named the majestic forest Timber Ridge.

The initial peaceful settlement of the Valley soon evaporated, and five years later Indians killed John McDowell. His remains lie today on the Great Path, or U.S. Rt. 11. Magdalena lived on, to see her descendants become famous soldiers, governors, surgeons, and educators. She helped tame a wilderness. With her third husband, the General John Bowyer, Magdalena lived through a Revolution that brought to birth the United States of America.

When the new county was formed out of Augusta County in 1778, John and Magdalena named it Rockbridge. They had visited a huge stone arch spanning a ravine to the south of their property and knew the name to be most fitting. In the entire nation, only one county bears the title of Rockbridge. They named the county seat Lexington, after the opening battle of the American Revolution in Lexington, Massachusetts, and built a new brick home at the edge of this new village. It stands yet on Thorn Hill. A historical marker on Rt. 251 tells the story.

Rockbridge County Scene

Lesson 2:
Life in These "Back Parts" of Virginia

In contrast to the history of Jamestown, there is no record of mass starvation among the pioneers of Virginia's back parts. More than a hundred years had passed since Jamestown. A government and commercial networks had been established, and agricultural practices were much improved. However, there are additional reasons for the contrast. Those first settlers had been more conscious of class. "Gentlemen" were not expected to do manual work. Ships from London would supply food whenever it could not be purchased from the natives. British sponsors would take care of the colony. Settlers would soon find gold to refill the empty ships for the return trip, they thought.

By the time frontiersmen moved into the western portion of Virginia, the dreams of gold had long since faded. These Scot-Irish immigrants came in quest of land and economic opportunity. Their mindset was different. Class lines were blurred. Upward social mobility had to be earned on the frontier. Every able body was expected to work. Settlers came south on the Great Path into Rockbridge with remarkable courage but pitifully few possessions. Some could afford packhorses; others carried all their possessions on their backs. Rifle and axe were the two major tools, along with iron cooking pots. Everything else would have to come from materials at hand.

Crucial questions arose every step of the way: Which plants can provide food, and which are deadly? How severe will the winters be? Sparkling streams are everywhere, but is the water safe for drinking? Where are the Indians who created all this open land? Did they die of some unseen disease lurking among these lovely hills? One of the most difficult questions was where to stop: Is there a better spot farther on, over the next ridge, or should we stay close to the others?

In 1737 the first Borden Grant settlers wasted no time. The McDowells and Houstons made their choices and put down roots. They built log cabins near the Great Path and began building a heritage of self-reliance. Other settlers followed, but many of them were less decisive. They lived in crude log cabins until they could be more certain of the right location. Cooking fires remained outdoors, Indian style. With time the pioneers brought the fire indoors, using chimneys made of mud and sticks, called wattle and daub. Larger more prominent homes were eventually made of logs, stone, or bricks, and safer chimneys were constructed of stone or brick.

Wildlife, which was plentiful, provided most of the food. Indian corn, wheat, rye, and oats were planted from the beginning, along with flax and fruit trees. Sugar maples produced abundant sweets long before honeybees were brought in. Wild chestnuts and native fruits comprised a large portion of the pioneer diet. Domestic farm animals were initially scarce, but very quickly large numbers of cattle and hogs roamed the countryside. Hemp, which could be turned into rope and cloth, was the cash crop. Flax was turned into linen. The process for both was labor intensive. Outer clothing was usually fashioned from animal skins, deer or cowhide. Wool could be processed into a valuable fabric, but there was a problem. Sheep loved the Rockbridge environment, but wolves loved sheep. Despite the legendary aversion to taxation, our ancestors in the back parts imposed a tax to pay for wolf head bounties.

With axe, adze, and auger, the pioneer constructed his dwelling and his furnishings. When sickness or injury occurred, home remedies were concocted from field and forest. Serious wounds were sewn shut, often by the victim himself. Almost every permanent homesite had a burial plot. Death was familiar. The meeting-house graveyard came as a later custom.

The Scot-Irish settlers did not require entertainment on the Rockbridge frontier. The primary social activity was "The Meeting," a Presbyterian worship service held whenever a preacher was available. During the first quarter century, such gatherings were possible only once a month or less often. Wilderness living did not diminish the educational standards for clergy, and as a result ministers were scarce.

In the late 1750s Rockbridge settlers (still a part of Augusta County) were caught up in panic after the French defeated British troops at Fort Duquesne. Everyone expected France to empower Indians in wiping out the entire American frontier, which was then considered British territory. The British established a line of official military forts along the western frontier. Within communities however, some homes and meeting houses were "fortified" as temporary places to gather for safety. Remarkable Presbyterian clergymen suddenly emerged with a military spirit. The Reverend Samuel Davies and the Reverend John Brown exhorted their people not to flee but to fortify. It worked. Small forts sprang up, some built of stone but most built of logs. There, families could gather in time of danger. Some of the meeting houses that met that need are today called Presbyterian churches, with such names as Augusta Stone, Oxford, Timber Ridge, and Providence.

Resolute families learned how to prevail during those frightening years, and they helped shape the course of American history. From 1755 to 1765 they stood up to every threat from the French and the Indians, and they survived. Their self-reliance hardened into an iron confidence. They knew they could take care of themselves. They would not be intimidated. No one, including their own king, would be allowed to take away liberty.

A decade later these Valley Presbyterians helped Thomas Jefferson write a fiery document that resulted in war with the Mother Country. We call that sheet of parchment the Declaration Of Independence. Historians tell us that our founding fathers were in the minority. Two-thirds of the American population opposed the declaration and the war for independence. They wanted England's protection. They respected royal rulers. They did not respect frontier rabble. After years of struggle, the minority was victorious. A new nation was born, offering liberty and justice for all.

Benjamin Franklin summed up our emerging philosophy in one famous slogan: "Those who would purchase security at the price of liberty deserve neither."

Oxford Church circa 1758

Lesson 3:
Forks of the James

As soon as the McDowells decided to become the first permanent residents on Borden's Grant (Rockbridge County) in 1737, they sent word back to Pennsylvania, Scotland, and Ireland, encouraging friends and relatives to join them. Here was virtually unlimited land, fertile and cheap, in a climate even more agreeable than the Old Country. Entire communities responded, pouring into Virginia's lovely valley. Most of these people had lived through hardship and religious discrimination and were desperate for a better life. They wanted land of their own, and they wanted free exercise of their own religion. They got both eventually, though some of them paid with their lives.

Most of the Rockbridge pioneers were Presbyterian. A few were Germans. Most were less than happy with the enforced religion of the government church. They did not object to the doctrines. What they despised was coercion. The established church in Virginia was Anglican, supported by taxes. Government officers punished anyone who failed to attend the services or pay the church assessments. By 1740 pious settlers were gathering for worship in Borden's Grant. They made no effort to adhere to the Book of Common Prayer. Their services were improvised and informal, often held under the shade of a tree. Although some of the more prominent names were appointed as vestrymen of the official state church, which gave them significant civil authority, their hearts were Presbyterian. Fiercely independent, they stood for self-government. Objecting to the heavy-handed rulings of the state church, they were labeled Dissenters.

East of the mountains, pastors who dared to question the style of the Anglican Church were seen as enemies of the government. They were fined, imprisoned, and scorned. Here on the dangerous frontier, things were different. There were no bishops protecting the Church of England. Settlers were compelled to pay church taxes, but no priests were telling them how and when to worship. Governor Gooch made a wise decision. He decreed that the Presbyterian dissenters should be unmolested among the mountains in these "back parts of Virginia." He understood that they served a purpose. They constituted a safeguard and barrier between tidewater planters and hostile Indians to the west.

Ironically, the sturdy backwoodsmen won the whole game. Those Scot-Irish Presbyterians survived. Back in England, Parliament was dealing with America's clamor for independence. Some did not refer to it as a Revolution; they called it the "Presbyterian Rebellion." So did aristocratic colonists east of the mountains. They considered themselves too civilized to resist England's church and England's rule. In contrast, stubborn Presbyterian fighters defied the British king. Against all odds, they triumphed over the strongest army in the world. Then they helped the new nation set up a government patterned specifically after the Presbyterian style. Finally, when the United States Constitution was written, Virginia's western leaders insisted that total freedom of religion be one of our guarantees. Never again would forcible taxation support any church. No government official would dictate sermon contents. Churches would be built wherever the people chose to build them, and they would no longer be called "meeting houses." The world came to understand a new kind of liberty, never before seen on the planet.

Early Rockbridge Christians, all of them dissenters, considered religion a vital part of life. They learned to avoid the word "church," so they had worshipped at their meeting houses. Along the Great Path in their valley, Providence Meeting House appeared, then Timber Grove, both of them north of the river fording at a spot later named Lexington. The Great Path crossed North River at a cleft in the rocks and pushed on. Hall's Meeting House arose at Whistle Creek. On Buffalo Creek, there was Falling Spring and Oxford. "Meeting House Lane" connected

Oxford Meeting House and a little settlement farther to the west later named Collierstown.

Old maps show the unfolding story. In 1735, cautious settlers had moved into the Beverley Manor. Two years later the Borden Grant appeared. Together these two pieces of land spanned at least forty miles in Virginia's Valley. The area was designated "The Irish Tract." Most of the families had names beginning with "Mac." As geography became more specific, the acreage of what is now Augusta County became known as "The Triple Forks Of the Shenandoah." "Forks Of The James" referred to virtually everything in present Rockbridge. It's a fitting name. Imagine viewing the topography from a seat in the sky. There below you is the great James River. Just before it breaks through the mountains on its way to Jamestown, it is joined by North (Maury) River, South River, Buffalo Creek, Kerrs Creek, Hays Creek, Mill Creek, and Moffetts Creek...all of them forks of the James.

A historian has to wonder if those waters carry uncommon chemistry. How else did "Forks Of The James" produce leadership out of all proportion to population or wealth or social status? Out of the unlikely "back parts" arose world-class soldiers, statesmen, educators, theologians, surgeons, and inventors. The steady stream of genius surprised and impressed a nation.

The little school at Timber Ridge Meeting House, with pastors John Brown and William Graham at the helm, evolved into Washington and Lee University. Where buffalo herds forded the north fork of the James, Virginia Military Institute arose in response to the vision of John Preston. On the south fork, a tinkerer by the name of "Mac" Cormick built a machine that brought on the global agricultural revolution. A few years earlier his young neighbor Archibald Alexander had learned skills under William Graham that enabled him to found Princeton Seminary. One of the McDowell sons became governor of Virginia. Another introduced abdominal surgery to the world. Sam Houston moved on from Timber Ridge to make history in Tennessee and Texas and to define the southwestern boundary of the United States. The mountain air and the sparkling waters of Rockbridge, blending with Presbyterian piety, obviously produced astonishing results.

Lesson 4:
Justice in Early Rockbridge

During the initial settling of what we now call Rockbridge County, people had to be self-reliant if they were to survive. Some of our ancestors would express astonished scorn at our dependence upon government institutions today. They did not expect government schools to educate their children. They would have been aghast if some agency tried to inspect food and drink in order to determine what should be fit for human consumption. Those strong Scot-Irish Presbyterians found it offensive when they were forced to allow roadways and gates for the benefit of travelers who needed to cross the area. They were never happy when taxed to pay for the operation of the established state church, which was not their chosen Presbyterian religion.

Even though this part of Virginia was a wild frontier, the culture was not lawless. People looked to the elders of the local Presbyterian meeting house for justice when matters could not be handled personally. Frontiersmen worked through their disputes, sometimes in rough-handed style. They soon learned that if they chose to fight the offensive neighbor, it was best done in private. Court records of Orange and Augusta, our first seats of public justice, indicate that fistfights were not acceptable either at church funerals or at the courthouse. Participants were fined. When we consider the difficulty of travel from here to Orange, on the other side of the Blue Ridge, it is easy to understand how the early settlers would have been motivated to settle disputes on their own, in the woods.

By 1778, fifty years after the first settlers arrived, Rockbridge County had its own court. John Bowyer, third husband of the lovely Magdalena, rode from Thorn Hill to preside over the first session held on April 7th at the home of Samuel Wallace, three miles to the east. It was a busy time for the new county. Our American Revolt, or War For Independence from Britain, was not going well. The court appointed Captains of militia. For the first time, the famous Liberty Hall Volunteers appeared in history. Who was their captain? William Graham, that remarkable Presbyterian preacher, founder of the school, which we know as Washington and Lee University. Tough Rockbridge boys helped turn the tide of war in the victorious battle of Guilford Court House.

The name of James Hall appears prominently in the record during the first weeks of the new court. He was an Indian fighter and soldier from Oxford Church. Hall and his friends were involved in the pivotal battles at Point Pleasant where Indians were ultimately defeated but at great cost to the militia. Many consider this October 1774 battle in West Virginia the first engagement of the American Revolution. When Chief Cornstalk was killed in 1777, James Hall, Hugh Galbraith, Malcolm McCown, and William Rowan were considered responsible. Our British enemies quite naturally made the most of the incident, hoping to use Indian hostility against the Americans. Governor Patrick Henry sensed the political implications, and from the safety of his office far from any frontier, Henry called for the perpetrators to be brought to trial. They were. General John Bowyer's brand-new court of Rockbridge found them not guilty of the murder charges. Furthermore, he helped appoint James Hall to the rank of militia captain. Those two men served together several times during the remainder of the Revolution and in the minds of many are considered American patriots.

By August of 1778 a new courthouse was under construction, not at the home of Samuel Wallace, but in the tiny village that Bowyer had named Lexington. The courthouse was small, only sixteen by twenty feet. A sheriff was appointed. The court also named several constables who were commissioned to settle minor cases in the outlying segments of Rockbridge.

A strong jail was built with the same dimensions as the new courthouse, but of huge logs squared to fourteen inches by fourteen inches throughout. Law and order had finally come to Rockbridge, the scenic area first described in unflattering terms as "the back parts of Virginia." The little court did its best to follow the pattern set in Williamsburg and Richmond. Over there, on the genteel side of the mountain, aristocratic planters had already learned to depend on government. They required tavern keepers to obtain a permit from the court, if liquor was to be sold. Rockbridge settlers did not welcome such an intrusion of government. One notable example was Mary McDowell Greenlee, feisty sister-in-law of Magdalena Bowyer. She served liquor and food at her tavern for years before there was any court in Rockbridge. When the new justices reminded her that a license would henceforth be required, she sent word back immediately telling them in caustic language exactly what they could do with their "permit."

The new court established rates to be charged for food and drink and lodging in our county. Each bed had a separate nightly fee, depending on how many travelers were sharing it, whether it provided straw or feather mattress, and whether sheets were available or not.

Punishments were excessive. Offenders were fined, jailed, whipped, and executed. An unbelievable number of women were sentenced to "twenty-five lashes on the bare back, well laid on." Men usually received an equal number of stripes if found guilty. In February of 1779 Catharine Coster, accused of stealing, was not proven guilty but was ordered to the whipping-post anyway for twenty-five lashes. Driving a wagon on the Sabbath brought a fine to William Gray. The Orange County court charged heavy fines for non-attendance at church. A few years later, in the hills of Rockbridge, you were allowed to skip church, as the established state church had been abolished. But no common labor was permitted on the Lord's Day. When the court gave people a choice between a fine and a whipping, many chose the whipping. Cash for meeting fines was obviously hard to earn in those days. Broken skin would heal, usually. Roger McCormick was sent to jail for speaking words of loyalty to the king of England. James Bailey was fined for referring to the federal legislature as the "damned Congress." For the first time in Rockbridge, money appeared as "dollars" instead of the British coin.

A determined imagination is required to construct a mental image of men and women being roped to a public whipping-post in the center of Lexington, their sensitive skin exposed and slashed with whips. The mere thought is revolting. However, even that punishment pales in comparison to the judgment rendered by the court in December of 1786. A slave named York was found guilty of killing Tom, a fellow slave. John Greenlee, high sheriff, was ordered to hang York until dead, then sever York's head and set it on a post for thirty days at the corner of Houston and Main streets as a solemn warning to all transgressors. Be aware, we are not describing Medieval Europe. This is Lexington, Virginia, the "Athens of the south," a mere two centuries ago. Were those the "good old days?" In some ways, perhaps. But I am happy that I will not likely be required under any circumstance to fulfill a duty as grisly as that assigned to Sheriff Greenlee.

Lesson 5:
The Lady Magdalena

I want to bring some recognition to the most under-appreciated heroine of Rockbridge, the matriarch of Borden's Grant. Her name is Magdalena. Born in Ulster, Ireland in 1715, she was the daughter of Michael and Mary Woods. In 1737 she came to America with her husband John McDowell and little son Samuel. They were not poor peasants. John was a land surveyor. Accompanied by several other members of the McDowell family, they made their way from Philadelphia into Virginia's wild valley. One evening as they camped near what is now named Raphine, a stranger approached. He introduced himself as Benjamin Borden. He told them, "I own one hundred thousand acres of this new land, but am not sure where it is. I need a surveyor."

John McDowell and Benjamin Borden quickly worked out a deal that was a bargain for both. The skillful surveyor managed to locate the boundaries for Borden, who in return deeded one percent of the tract to McDowell. John and Magdalena chose their one thousand acres between present-day Fairfield and Timber Ridge. They built a log house, stained red. Magdalena gave birth to two more children, James and Sarah. After planting and harvesting crops of corn and hemp, the couple sent word to other relatives, urging them to come to this frontier where land was low-priced but fruitful. Many did, coming from the old country and also from the coasts of America. Magdalena's brother Richard settled at the western edge of present-day Lexington. "Woods Creek," running through the town, was named for him. Magdalena's sister Sarah married Joseph Lapsley and settled on Whistle Creek a few miles farther to the west. Richard Woods and Joseph Lapsley both left distinguished legacies in Rockbridge history. So did Magdalena's other sister Martha, who married Peter Wallace. Their line produced "Big Foot Wallace," a "mountain man" who made history in Texas and whose fame is announced on the historic plaque at the corner of Main and Houston Streets in Lexington.

In December of 1742, Woods and Lapsley were part of John McDowell's militia that was called out to escort a troublesome party of Indians away from the nervous settlers. The operation turned tragic at the junction of the James and Maury Rivers, near the place now named Glasgow. A battle suddenly erupted, and young Captain McDowell, riding at the head of the party, was instantly killed. Lapsley and Woods brought his body back to Magdalena, who washed away the blood and buried him beside their home. The spot is to this day called "The McDowell Graveyard." It is a bricked-in lot beside U.S. Rt. 11 and is the resting place of John and other members of the notable family. Several Virginia historic markers stand near the site.

Benjamin Borden Jr. courted the widow. His father had died, leaving him as the new owner of the Borden Grant. Magdalena is described in old documents as a ravishing beauty. Her sister-in-law, Mary McDowell Greenlee, states in official court records that "Magdalena, mounted upon a white stallion, would be dressed in a green velvet riding habit that fell to the ground. Her hat was adorned with twelve ostrich plumes." Young Benjamin Borden finally won the hand of the lovely widow who at first spurned his advances. They were married in 1744 at Timber Grove Meeting House, the forerunner of Timber Ridge Church. Ben and Magdalena produced two daughters, Martha and Hannah. They continued to live at the "Red House" until 1753. Sadly, during that year both Benjamin and little Hannah died of smallpox.

Our remarkable heroine kept the home intact. She now owned and managed an enormous estate. She ran the huge farm. She cared for her children. She made contracts with the stream of settlers purchasing land from Borden's Grant. Rich and beautiful, she was nevertheless lonely, and she needed help. Magdalena caught the eye of John Bowyer, a strapping educator recently arrived in the area. They were married soon after the first meeting. Was it a marriage made in heaven? Maybe. It certainly endured, lasting for the remainder of Magdalena's long life.

Magdalena's new husband gave up teaching. Amazingly, John Bowyer proved to be a genius at managing wealth, first Magdalena's, then theirs, and finally his own. Bowyer wanted to put some distance between him and the McDowell graveyard. Since Magdalena owned most of the Rockbridge area, they had hundreds of hilltops on which to build. Instead, with her money and her blessing, they purchased a large tract of land near Liberty Hall. Being Presbyterian, they knew the owner...He was the Reverend Alexander Craighead, one of the first pastors in the valley. Craighead had named his place "Mispeh" which in Hebrew translates to "Watchtower Hill." On a scenic crest of Mispeh, John and Magdalena built their brick house that stands today only a few yards from the new home of another Presbyterian parson, the author of this history lesson. Magdalena changed the name to "Thorn Hill." Her husband John gave the name "Lexington" to the village below their home. Together, in 1787 they named the new county "Rockbridge."

Magdalena died in 1796. She probably lies in "the sacred grove of perfumed lilacs" as someone has described the family graveyard on Thorn Hill, but no one can be sure. There is no marker, and no records document her burial site.

Magdalena's eighty-one years were extraordinary. She was one of the first pioneer women in our valley and without question the most attractive. Her third husband rose to the rank of general in the Revolutionary War. He was the first presiding judge in Rockbridge. John Bowyer served in virtually every branch of government. He was a strong supporter of the college in Lexington. Patrick Henry and Thomas Jefferson were his close friends.

Marvelous Magdalena took part in the birth of our nation. She helped tame a fruitful wilderness. She was a survivor. Her children honored her, and many of them became famous. She saw one grandson become governor of Virginia. Governor McDowell's daughter Sally married Oxford's pastor, John Miller, and together they occupied the mansion in Lexington named "Col Alto." Another grandson achieved worldwide fame as "the father of abdominal surgery."

We do well to remember such a gallant lady. That is why my wife Ellen and I have named our hilltop not "Mispeh" nor "Thorn Hill" but "Magdalena," to honor this extraordinary woman.

Magdalena

Lesson 6:
Indians in Old Virginia

The painful story of our Native Americans evokes a pang of guilt. We wish it could be rewritten. The opening chapter begins well enough, with high hope and good intentions. English kings granted permission for adventurers to settle on the shores of Virginia with one very specific provision: they were to "Christianize the Indians, live peaceably among them, and bring to the savages the blessings of civilization." It was a noble goal that did not work out, despite enormous effort.

In the years 1607 to 1618, ten thousand acres had been set aside in a place called Henrico for building a college and seminary, where Indians could learn the white man's religion and culture. Anglican priests immediately began communicants' classes for Indian adults and children. It was in keeping with the charter, to the glory of God and in honor of the head of the church, the King of England. A powerful Indian leader named Opechankanough brought his braves in, presumably to learn the new faith. Despite some uneasiness between the two cultures and an occasional fight, the future seemed promising. The natives taught the inept settlers how to grow corn, how to fish, and how to smoke tobacco. The starvation years passed. Virginia plantations proved fruitful. December 4, 1619, was established as a Day Of Thanksgiving, two years before what is now erroneously called the "First Thanksgiving" at Plymouth, Massachusetts. The celebration was established at Berkeley Hundred in Virginia, on the James River. Things seemed to be going well.

However, there were no converts. The Native Americans did not care for the customs and habits and religion of the newcomers. An exception was Pocohantas, daughter of the famous chief Powhatan. As far as I can determine, this remarkable lady is one of the very few Indians to receive Christian baptism in early America. She wanted to marry John Rolfe, and an essential requirement was that she join the church. She complied.

In March of 1622, the wily Opechankanough showed his true intentions. His pretense at becoming Christian was nothing more than a plot to eradicate every white settler. He and his men conducted a well-planned massacre, killing hundreds of white men, women, and children. The terrible slaughter turned the tide, but not in the way the Indians had expected. The survivors, few as they were, rallied...wiser and more determined. Conversion of Indians was virtually abandoned. The earnest whites who had labored diligently in and for the college were all murdered on that March day, and the college expired with them. New goals were adopted in dealing with the natives, and those goals prevailed. Killing replaced conversion; extermination replaced education. Peaceful coexistence became a lost dream. Sadly, the first chapter closed on a bitter note.

More than a century later, settlers came across the mountains and began setting their homesteads in the Valley of Virginia. Although there were vague understandings that this was the "Indian side of the boundary," no natives were in sight. Here were open fields and lush pastures, seemingly deserted after centuries of Indian habitation. Why had the tribes moved out?

Contrary to what I was taught as a child, this land was not totally covered in virgin forest when the white settlers arrived. Indians had cultivated fields of corn. They had transformed much of the land into buffalo pasture by burning vast areas every year. If everything were wooded, there would have been no herds of buffalo and Buffalo Creek would be called by some other name.

The Scot-Irish settlers wondered if the non-resident Iroquois still claimed ownership of this valley. Meeting houses were constructed, one of which stood in front of Oxford Church. It was built of sturdy logs. We have no evidence that the structure was ever used in defense against Indian attack. We do know that it was where our forefathers gathered to worship God. Many of the settlers lived out their lives without so much as glimpsing a Native American, although small bands of hunters and warriors regularly passed through. Much of the Virginia Valley remained unmolested by Indians.

There were exceptions. In 1742 John McDowell, husband of Magdalena, was killed near the mouth of the Maury River, along with several of his militiamen. They were attempting to escort approximately thirty Indians out of Rockbridge's settled area. In 1759 and again in 1763, Shawnees attacked settlers in Kerrs Creek, killing and capturing as many as one hundred victims. Some historians set the number much lower. Surprisingly, no official records give account of either raid, leaving the details open to speculation.

Oren Morton in his *History Of Rockbridge County* concludes that Indians resented the settlers' desecration of ancient holy sites and burial mounds. Although natives no longer lived here, they made regular pilgrimages to honor their sacred ancestors. Morton speculates that the callous attitude of the white settlers was too offensive to ignore and brought on attacks. Morton writes of large burial mounds at Hays Creek, Glasgow, and Buffalo, all of which had been leveled by agriculture prior to 1920.

Stone artifacts are discovered with regularity in Rockbridge. All such tools predate the arrival of our European ancestors. Some of the implements may be tens of thousands of years old. The well-ordered gravemounds, the domestic stone tools, and the open meadows for corn and buffalo all prove that other people lived here many centuries ago. They revered the awesome hills, the sparkling waters, and the fertile valleys. Here they raised their children. Here they had their dances and held their powwows in honor of the Great Spirit. It was their labor that paved the way for settlement by our ancestors. It suggests to me that we owe them something, not the least of which would be respect and understanding.

I too love this land, nature's paradise...the most beautiful place on earth. When I roam the mountains behind Oxford Church, I enjoy the mental game of reconstructing history. For the past quarter-millennium my own race and culture have lived and labored here. Long before, there were the Indians. The land is not mine, even though my name is on the deed. The Great Spirit loaned this country to the Red Man, who is long since gone. Now it is my turn. The same Great Spirit has loaned it to me for a few years, to enjoy while I live.

Lesson 7:
The Reverend William Graham: Founder of W&L

Oxford Church has been served by some legendary pastors. One of them was William Graham. Although he suffered heartbreak here, as did at least two other early pastors of Oxford, the pain did not diminish his achievements. Graham was born in 1746, in Paxton Township Pennsylvania, the fifth of twelve children. He was a farm boy and developed survival skills early in life. Threats of Indian attacks taught him how to be armed and ready for anything. At age twenty-one he underwent a spiritual awakening and decided to enter the Presbyterian ministry. Enrolling in what was then the College of New Jersey (later named Princeton), he graduated with high honors in the class of 1773. What a class! Of the twenty-nine graduates, twenty-three became pastors, three were state governors, and four were college presidents. Two of those pastors served Oxford Church.

William Graham

Upon graduation William Graham immediately accepted a position as head of Augusta Academy, the classical Presbyterian school located south of Staunton in the Valley of Virginia. The academy shortly moved to Fairfield and then to Timber Ridge, both locations in Rockbridge County. By 1776 Graham had changed the name to Liberty Hall Academy in honor of the American Revolution. During those early years, Graham's mentor was Rev. John Brown, another brilliant educator and pastor of Timber Ridge and New Providence churches. When John Brown resigned as pastor of Timber Ridge, Graham became pastor of both Timber

Ridge and Hall's Meeting House, in addition to his teaching position at Liberty Hall. Historians are unanimous in assessing William Graham's ability as a brilliant instructor. He taught the young farmers' sons classical Latin, Greek, mathematics, literature, and all known science of the day. He created some of his own textbooks from notes he had written while studying under Rev. John Witherspoon, the noted Presbyterian pastor who signed our Declaration Of Independence.

Heartbreak came to Graham when he fell in love with the boss's daughter, Elizabeth Brown. The girl's mother despised Graham. The romance never had a chance. Elizabeth turned her attention to Samuel McCorkle, Oxford's pastor, who promptly fell desperately in love with her. But Elizabeth broke McCorkle's heart too, by suddenly marrying Rev. Thomas Craighead, whose father owned five hundred acres including Thorn Hill where my own new home stands today. My study of Virginia's frontier tells me that young Presbyterian pastors had complicated love issues.

William Graham and John Brown kept their academy at Timber Ridge alive through the troubled years of the American Revolution. Both were strong teachers. The sturdy farm boys who sat at their feet were obviously gifted students. The little wartime classroom sent out two of its students to preside over the highest courts of the nation. Four served in state legislatures, and four served in Congress. Another lad was successful in establishing several colleges of international fame. My own childhood was spent in the Timber Ridge area, but not once was the stellar performance of Graham and his school mentioned in my presence. Today this seems odd. It helps spur me to write these short history lessons in an effort to keep alive some of our remarkable heritage.

Success inspired William Graham. He envisioned a college, something more impressive than his little log academy on the Ridge. His older partner John Brown disagreed. "We're doing a great job; let well enough alone," was Brown's reasonable attitude. The two scholars parted company. Rev. Graham moved to Lexington, bought a farm in hopes of improving his financial situation, and for a brief time continued to teach occasionally at the Timber Ridge location. So great was the desire for his instruction, young men descended upon the farm. Some of them actually moved in with Graham and his wife, Mary Kerr. By 1782 the eager students had, in effect, moved the school from Timber Ridge to Lexington. First he taught them in his home. Then a small building was erected on land donated from his farm. By 1794 an impressive stone structure was built and occupied, the ruins of which yet stand on the west edge of Washington and Lee University campus. Liberty Hall, thanks to the genius and generosity of William Graham, had become a college. It was supported and staffed by the Presbyterians of Virginia. Furthermore, it had evolved into a theological seminary as well, turning out such giants as Dr. Moses Hoge, Rev. Samuel Houston, Dr. George Baxter, and Dr. Archibald Alexander.

William Graham set up a "collegiate connection" between Oxford, Timber Ridge, Hall's, and the new meeting house he had

William Graham's grave on east side of Lee Chapel on the
Washington and Lee University campus.

established in Lexington. He and his other teachers at Liberty Hall filled the four pulpits with some help from his divinity students.

It is not surprising to learn that this energetic Presbyterian eventually suffered signs of exhaustion. Just take a look at all he was doing:

1. He ran a farm to support his family and his school.
2. He founded what is now Washington and Lee University, personally filling the position of head teacher and administrator for more than twenty years.
3. He was responsible for building the stone church at Hall's Meeting House (now called "Old Monmouth"). He built the first Presbyterian church in Lexington. He provided the vision for building Oxford's stone church.
4. He assisted Patrick Henry and Thomas Jefferson in bringing total religious liberty to Virginia.
5. He served as captain of militia on our frontier at the same time he was minister of the Prince of Peace.
6. He mastered and taught virtually every subject known in America, plus one of his own creation, "mental philosophy," now recognized as "psychology."
7. He inspired his pupils to attain national fame as political leaders, educators, pastors, inventors, and scholars.
8. He persuaded Gen. George Washington to make an incredible donation to Liberty Hall Seminary in Rockbridge County.

While the school seemed secure at last, Graham himself entered a mid-life crisis. He resigned his positions with the college and the churches. He invested everything in a land venture in western Virginia and lost it all. Riding to Richmond in an attempt to sort things out legally, his exposure to bad weather brought on pneumonia and death.

Only fifty-three years old, Graham left his wife and six children destitute. One hundred and twelve years later his remains were finally returned to Lexington.

As you enter Lee Chapel in 2007, there are two graves in the grass outside. The grave on the left side of the chapel is that of William Graham. Gen. Robert E. Lee's horse Traveller occupies the grave on the right side. Perhaps some day the university will do more to honor its single-handed founder. When I visit the campus, I find fresh flowers regularly placed on Traveller's grave, but I have never seen blossoms on the grave of Graham, our unloved hero. "Unloved" is a word that seems to fit. In all my research, not once have I found William Graham described as "beloved." Admired, yes. Respected, yes. Feared, yes. Loved, no. Everyone perceived him as brilliant. He seemed to share that assessment. Other peoples' advice meant little or nothing to him. When detractors scorned him for his ill-fated attempt to set up a new state in what is now Tennessee, Graham responded with such scathing sarcasm that they complained to Presbytery. He was tried for "comments unbecoming a minister of the gospel." Not surprisingly for a man who won every debate, Graham was found "not guilty." His caustic language was perhaps justified, but it did not win friends. To be "king of the mountain" is to be a lonely man.

Soften that loneliness for our hero. Visit his modest grave. Thank William Graham for his astounding contribution to our churches, our county, and our nation.

Lesson 8:
Captain James Hall: American Patriot

Perhaps the most notable permanent resident of Oxford cemetery is James Hall. He lived within sight of Oxford church in the house on the hill. His wife was Martha Gilmore, and both of them were born in America, in Virginia, in the Borden Grant area now known as Rockbridge County. By 1770, James and Martha had established their home on Buffalo Creek where their family grew and multiplied. James has another special connection to Oxford Church—his beautiful sister Mary was the young bride of the Reverend Samuel Houston, an Oxford pastor some years later.

From his earliest years, James Hall had difficulties with the Indians. He was acutely aware of the never-ending danger. The Gilmore family on Kerrs Creek had been slaughtered, with Mrs. Gilmore carried away in captivity. James and Martha, now living on the raw edge of the frontier, probably found little comfort in the fact that the Oxford meeting house near the edge of their farm served as the community's log fort and protection in case of Indian attack.

Constant threats from Indians, the French, and finally British enemies compelled young James Hall to become a warrior. He and his militia from Buffalo were in the thick of it at Point Pleasant in 1774. There on the banks of the Ohio River, present day West Virginia, a memorable battle took place. Many historians consider it the actual beginning of America's Revolutionary War. A confederation of Indian tribes led by a Shawnee chief, Conesqua (pronounced "cone-es-kwa"), was determined to drive out the settlers once and for all. Thanks to the valor of our Virginia Militia, the battle of Point Pleasant was a discouraging defeat finally for the Indians. Those Indians called these Virginia soldiers Long Knives, and those soldiers gave another name to Conesqua. They called him Cornstalk, which approximated the actual meaning of his Indian proper name. Chief Cornstalk was unquestionably one of the strongest Indian leaders of the eighteenth century and was responsible for many of the deadly raids against settlers in the Valley of Virginia. The very mention of Cornstalk's name struck fear in the hearts of our forefathers and mothers.

With Captain Hall, however, the emotion was not fear but rather defiance and fury. At the Point Pleasant Battle many soldiers died, including Colonel Charles Lewis. Another illustrious leader from our area, Colonel William Fleming, was badly wounded. Three years later in 1777, Hall and his men were ordered back to Point Pleasant for another confrontation. Chief Cornstalk, recognizing that he was going to get whipped, came to the fort claiming to be a negotiator for peace. His son and two other Indian tribal leaders joined him. Captain Hall and the men from Oxford had no confidence in such discussions. They felt the entire assembly was a trick and a farce, perhaps even a trap. But they waited. While they waited, two of Hall's soldiers went turkey hunting. Some Indians attacked them, killing and scalping one—a private whose name was Gilmore. The surviving soldier dashed back to the fort with this bad news for Captain Hall. Upon recovering the badly mutilated body of Gilmore, who was probably a relative of Hall's wife, the rage was uncontrollable. It was proof to Hall and his men that the peace party was nothing short of deception. Grabbing their rifles, they swiftly executed the four Indians. To this day people disagree on whether that killing was justified or simply cold-blooded murder. Only Cornstalk would be able to settle that argument, as only Cornstalk knew his own true motives.

From all directions, loud voices clamored for justice: "Captain Hall must be brought to trial!" Patrick Henry, Governor of Virginia, publicly condemned the killings. From the safety of his office, hundreds of miles from Indian danger, one can only wonder at our famous governor's judgment. But a trial was held. Hall and two of his men were indicted for murder. Conditions proved favorable for the soldiers. Rockbridge County had just been established in 1778, so the men would be tried in their home community. That first court was held in the home of Samuel Wallace, a mile or so east of Lexington. The presiding officer, fortunately, was Gen. John Bowyer, Magdalena's husband and past commander of Hall and his company. He would be the commander again in more battles of the Revolution with Hall and his troops under him.

Captain Hall was found not guilty. He was the first man in Rockbridge County to be tried and acquitted for murder. He lies now right outside our church's front door near his beloved farm. I would want to ask, if I could get his attention for only a moment, "Captain Hall, would you do it again? Or do you have regrets?"

Lesson 9:
Who was Chief Cornstalk?

When our beautiful valley was becoming home to our Presbyterian ancestors, Indians did not inhabit it. The land had large prairies, having been burned each autumn by Indian hunting parties in order to attract buffalo herds. To the Scot-Irish this land looked like God's gift...a fertile farming area, free for the taking...but Indians perceived the rich valley as their happy hunting ground.

Some Indian leaders saw the stream of settlers as an invasion that must be stopped. One of these was the great emperor Pontiac, chief of the Ottawas. A young man who was born about 1720 took Chief Pontiac as his own role model. The young Indian's name as Conesqua, which in Indian means "blade of corn." The settlers had difficulty with pronunciation, so they called him Cornstalk and the nickname stuck to this day.

Cornstalk rose in prominence to become a Shawnee Chief. He was famous for his strength, his size, his good looks, his bravery, and his spoken eloquence. Although he was beloved by his own people, Cornstalk proved to be a terrible menace to the settlers. He is believed to be responsible for many raids that killed settlers off so steadily as to threaten total annihilation of the whites. Settlements in Greenbrier, Kerrs Creek, and Abbs Valley, for example, were virtually wiped out.

By 1774, Chief Cornstalk had put together a confederation of tribes producing the mightiest Indian armed force ever seen on our continent. The Virginia militia finally confronted Cornstalk's army at Point Pleasant where the Ohio and Kanawha Rivers merge. The Indians were defeated, but at great cost to our army. More than seventy Virginia soldiers are buried there, most of them from right here in this valley.

In 1777, at the same strategic location, history was about to be repeated. Both sides had mustered impressive forces. Cornstalk realized the risks and offered to negotiate, perhaps in good faith or perhaps as a trap...we do not know. But, when during the parley an attack on some white soldiers left one dead, militia from Oxford had had more than enough. They swiftly executed Cornstalk along with his son and two other Indian leaders. By this time in our history, war with Great Britain had been underway for two years. The British and others used Cornstalk's execution to portray Americans as savage intruders who should be driven out or annihilated, or at least subdued.

The issues are complicated. Who was right? Who was wrong? That was being debated while the Revolutionary War was going on right here in Virginia. Through the ages and up to the present, the answers vary. As always, some perceive America as a relentless, aggressor, even as the Great Satan. Others view our nation as noble, generous, and blessed by God. Obviously you have a choice. You can choose which attitude you want to take. You can choose which to believe, whether you are considering the war in Iraq today or the character of Chief Cornstalk in 1777.

The Shawnee Chief Cornstalk lies buried at Point Pleasant, West Virginia, in the Tu-Endue-Wei Park. A stone monument marks his grave. Most of our American patriots are buried without surviving markers. We have quite a number of those soldiers in our own Oxford Church cemetery. One of those unmarked graves belongs to Captain James Hall, leader of the Oxford militia at Point Pleasant in 1774 and again in 1777 when Cornstalk was killed. However, in 2008, a bronze tablet was set on a large stone in Oxford cemetery, memorializing Captain Hall.

After James Hall's trial and acquittal for his involvement in Cornstalk's death, he was commissioned again as an officer in the Revolutionary War serving under Gen. John Bowyer of Thorn Hill, Lexington, Virginia. His final years were spent peacefully right here farming the lovely fields near our church. Other soldiers grew old beside him. One of them was his brave brother-in-law, the Reverend Samuel Houston who preached in what was then the stone church of Oxford. No doubt they sat together companionably before the fireplace in Hall's home on many long winter evenings, and perhaps the conversation occasionally brought forth the name of an Indian, Chief Cornstalk, whose ghost was always hovering near.

LESSON 10:
The Reverend Samuel Houston

The Houston name was glowing with valor long before appearing in the Valley of Virginia. Exploits such as the Siege of Londonderry in 1688 involved heroic Houstons. Centuries earlier in the year 1066, William the Conqueror relied heavily on one of the Norman knights, Sir Hugh de Padivan, whom he rewarded with an estate on the Scottish border. The castle and land came to be known as "Hugh's Town," a name much easier to pronounce. From then on the clan has been "Houston." Their religion was Presbyterian, putting them at odds with the Church of Ireland. Economic incentives led them to Ireland where discrimination, rising rents, and famine pushed them onward to America.

On a remarkable voyage to the New World in 1729, the Houstons and McDowells had to fight for their lives. The captain and crew intended to rob them of their valuables, knowing that those heavy trunks contained family silver and gold from the sale of belongings in Ireland. Our heroes prevailed. They took over the ship, sailed into Philadelphia, unloaded their possessions, and then returned the keys to the shackled crew. Discrimination had honed and hardened our ancestors. It gave them skills for taming the wild frontier of Virginia's "back parts," as eastern planters called this area.

The Houston and McDowell families were the first to settle and stay in Borden's Grant, now called Rockbridge County. They arrived in 1737, choosing as their homesteads large parcels of land in what is now the Fairfield, Brownsburg, and Timber Ridge area. The subject of this lesson, Reverend Samuel Houston, was born in 1758 and grew to adulthood at the New Providence Presbyterian Church, which stood near the front door of his home. An interesting historical note is that his cousin, Gen. Sam Houston, one generation later, was born and reared near the door of Timber Ridge Presbyterian Church. Both men became famous, suggesting that life near a Presbyterian church can be a positive influence on children.

Little Samuel was a frail child. More than once his parents made preparations for his death, but the Houston genetics finally triumphed. He grew into strong manhood. Young Samuel received his elementary education first at home and then at Mount Pleasant Academy near present-day Fairfield. Reverend John Brown, pastor of Timber Ridge and New Providence Churches, was the schoolmaster. Most of the students were members of those two churches. Samuel Houston, with some interruptions, remained a pupil throughout notable historic events: The American Revolutionary War, the relocation of the school to Timber Ridge, and the change in name from Mount Pleasant Academy to Liberty Hall. During those years the illustrious William Graham appeared and succeeded John Brown as schoolmaster.

By 1792, that school was in Lexington and had been renamed Washington College. Rev. Samuel Houston was clerk of the college's board of trustees. He had seen the school grow from a small log house into an academy and then into a college and theological seminary. He had a part in securing the gift from George Washington that proved pivotal in the survival of the institution we now know as Washington and Lee University. Rev. Houston had received all his formal schooling through only one line of instructors, but it was obviously adequate. Presbytery licensed him as a minister in the early 1780s, and he became renowned as a scholar on Virginia's frontier. The Revolutionary War turned him into a warrior for at least one year. Historical records distinguish Samuel Houston as "bravest of the brave" during the famous Battle of Guilford Courthouse, where the militia faced British forces under General Cornwallis.

Houston's first pastoral assignment was in Tennessee. Today a historic marker stands beside the highway near Kingsport declaring him to be the "first Presbyterian minister ever ordained in Tennessee." His church was named Providence in honor of the home church here in Rockbridge. Samuel married Mary Hall, a beautiful Oxford girl with striking eyes...one blue, the other jet-black. Mary's famous brother, Captain James Hall, lies in a grave just outside our church door. Tragically, when Samuel returned home from a presbytery meeting in Virginia, he found his bride seriously ill with a fever, and she soon died in his arms. Following Mary's death, Reverend Houston maintained close contact with the Hall family, visiting them often from Tennessee, and even more often after he moved back to Virginia. It was Samuel Houston who conducted the funeral for Captain James Hall on Oxford's hill.

In Tennessee, Houston made history as a pastor, but he is also remembered for his leadership in the movement to establish Frankland, or Franklin, as a separate state. The effort failed after bitter demonstrations, one of which involved burning effigies of Rev. Houston and Rev. William Graham. It was time to come home. In the summer of 1788 Houston moved to the Natural Bridge area, taking charge of Falling Spring, High Bridge, and Oxford Churches. By 1794 he had chosen another Rockbridge beauty as his wife, Margaret Walker. From then on, his life seems to have been full and fruitful. The couple bought six hundred acres of rich farmland watered by Cedar Creek and Broad Creek, lying on the flank of Short Hill Mountain. The next four years were busy for Houston. He built new churches at both Falling Spring and High Bridge, and he constructed a large home where he conducted a theological seminary and an academy, or high school.

The pastor's accomplishments were phenomenal. While raising distinguished children, he was somehow able to teach theology and the classics for budding pastors. He managed model farms and wrote agricultural literature for publication throughout our new country. Samuel preached several times each week. He performed more weddings than any other pastor of his day. Many of those marriages were solemnized on the crest of Short Hill, midway between Oxford and Rural Valley, as his home and school were named. (Can you imagine young couples in love, atop our soaring mountain, hearing those magic words: "I now pronounce you man and wife?") Houston owned several slaves. With their help he invented and patented a threshing machine, as well as a winnowing machine. His ideas, techniques, and machines were far ahead of the current agriculture of his day.

Rev. Houston became totally blind in his last years, sometimes preaching without realizing he had faced away from his congregation during the sermon. He is the pastor who baptized Mary Moore after her Indian captivity and married her to the Reverend Samuel Brown of New Providence. The marriage broke the heart of Daniel Blain, who thought she would become his wife. Blain was pastor of Oxford at the time, in 1798.

Samuel Houston died in 1839 at the age of eighty-one. His wife Margaret died in 1854. Both of them lie in High Bridge Cemetery, their graves partially covered by more recent additions to the church structure. The venerable scholar's last breath was taken as he was preparing a sermon for the coming Sabbath. Hauntingly, the text and title of that sermon is: "He that is dead, yet speaketh."

Try to envision this multi-faceted frontier pastor. He is described as handsome, erect, square-shouldered, and strong. He was meticulously dressed from head to toe in the finest custom-made apparel Lexington craftsmen could offer. Whenever his signature was required, he signed his name "Samuel Houston, VDM." The letters stand for the Latin *Verbum Dei Magister*, minister of the word of God.

Lesson 11:
Presbyterians Had Some Problems

Most of us think our Scot-Irish ancestors attending Oxford Meeting House were stiff, stern, stubborn, strict, silent, serious, and strong. Usually they were. After all, they were newcomers to this promised land where hardship and danger challenged them daily. This frontier offered a priceless treasure called liberty. But to enjoy liberty, one first had to survive. Those settlers needed God's help, and they knew it. Religion became serious business, and places for worship were constructed as a priority.

By the late 1750s Upper Buffalo had a log meeting house that doubled as a temporary fort. Preachers were scarce, but the people gathered with or without a pastor to call upon God. In the Valley of Virginia, most people were Presbyterian despite the fact that the official government church was Anglican. Only the Church of England clergy were licensed to preach and perform weddings as official representatives of the government. In the Valley, dissenters such as Presbyterians, Lutherans, German Reformed, and Brethren were given tolerance in return for their settlement on the western frontier.

Oxford Church circa 1810

Presbyterians were thus outsiders. They bonded and stiffened and stood together facing hostile Indians on one side and a less-than-friendly government church on the other. Independence became their trademark. Mentally, politically, commercially, and religiously they were forced to look out for themselves. Surprisingly, their convictions prevailed. America ultimately took on a Presbyterian form of representative government, under God, with liberty and justice for all, regardless of birth or status. We are indebted to our sturdy forbears. We can be justly proud to remember and to follow them. Still, Presbyterians had some problems. They could agree on basic matters of doctrine, but a big question remained: How should a Christian behave when moved and touched by Almighty God?

The Presbyterian parson was invariably educated to the very highest level. Worship tended toward solemnity and dignity. However, sermons in early America usually emphasized the awful prospect of hell, to the point of terror. Sometimes emotions were strained beyond the breaking point. Listeners would burst into sobs, then screams, crying out for God's mercy, which alone could save them from dropping into the flaming pit of hell. An especially guilty conscience would cause convulsions—wild bodily jerks followed by vigorous dancing, fits, and fainting. At Hall's Meeting House on Whistle Creek, where Oxford Church has her roots, one woman fell out the door and rolled some one hundred yards in her Sunday finery. Such an exhibit is surely impressive, even when powered by the Holy Spirit (see Sander's *History of New Monmouth Presbyterian Church*, p. 40).

Could such behavior be truly from God? Different churchmen had different answers. The venerable John Brown, distinguished pastor at Timber Ridge and New Providence, emphatically said, "No!" The gyrations and displays were embarrassing and deplorable, not to be tolerated in any decent Christian assembly. The Reverend William Graham, pastor of Oxford and Hall's, was more generous. Graham was perhaps the first psychiatrist in Virginia. He was deeply interested in the workings of the human mind. Brilliant in scholarship, Graham advised his flock to be open-minded, reminding them that God works in mysterious ways. Other religious leaders encouraged the exciting exhibitions, insisting that no one could claim true conversion without such an experience.

The Presbyterians split, at the very point in history where they desperately needed to present a united front. One faction was named "Old Side" and stood for dignity, decorum, and finely honed intelligence. The other faction was called "New Side" and encouraged visible, emotional evidence of "born again" religion. The New Side revivalism brought people to church. Fear of a fiery hell is an effective motivator. It seems that many people want to be terrorized, then saved. In America, religion had lost some urgency following the Revolutionary War. Fashionable young people scorned the stuffed shirts of Presbyterianism. The New Side helped turn that tide.

William Graham, while preaching at Hall's (now New Monmouth) one Sunday afternoon had his service rudely interrupted. Three young men were outside, slamming rocks against the church walls and harassing the congregation. When rebuked, one of them shouted defiantly at the horrified worshippers, "I will never set foot in this house of fools!" Several weeks later that man fell from his barn loft and died instantly. Graham preached the funeral, sparing no venom. He made the listeners tremble. Shortly thereafter another of the young men was killed in a hunting accident a few days after his marriage. That same year the third man fell from his horse and died in agony with spinal injuries. Even the hardened skeptics took notice and joined Graham's church. Archibald Alexander, a Rockbridge lad who became famous as the founder of Princeton Theological Seminary, wrote of the incident, concluding, "Verily there is a God in heaven who demands reverence."

Before 1900, the New Side and Old Side got back together in an uneasy truce, but the question still remains unsettled. Which approach leads toward heaven and can keep you away from hell? It is more than a life or death question...it has to do with eternity.

As a bored teenager, I would hide in the honeysuckle to observe Pentecostal revivals at a little church near my home. They were loud, physical, and deliciously unpredictable. Men would shout, "Amen!" Large country women would roll in the aisles, often barking like dogs. Singing, weeping voices filled the night air. By comparison, the sober, solemn worship at my own church seemed tepid and pale, but somehow I preferred it that way.

The Presbyterian denomination tries to make room for differences of opinion within their ranks. At Oxford Church we still benefit from the cool genius of William Graham these two hundred years later. Rarely do we see anybody rolling in the aisles, but we do things never allowed in those early days. We clap our hands in hearty applause. We speak "Amen," but gently. We sing a hymn brought to us by the Shakers who derived their name from bodily exercises arising from true religion. The appealing hymn says, "Dance, then, wherever you may be. I am the Lord of the dance, said He [Christ]. I'll lead you all in the dance, said He." Old Siders would find the hymn offensive. They would break away and build a separate church to avoid the sacrilege. How do I know? They did precisely that, more than once, in little Rockbridge County, a veritable hatchery of Presbyterians.

Lesson 12:
Complicated Love: Oxford's Early Pastors

I have to wonder: Did other churches have the same problem as Oxford? Her first pastors were not lucky in love. The men were highly trained. They were admired as political and intellectual leaders. One would assume that the unmarried Presbyterian parson could write his own ticket in the matter of choosing a life mate, especially here in the "back parts" of Virginia. Such was not always the case at Oxford.

William Graham was probably the most intellectually gifted person who ever lived in our area. Almost single-handedly Graham conceived and founded the school now known as Washington and Lee University. He was a powerful speaker. So far as I can determine, he never lost a debate. When Graham was pastor at Oxford, he was married to Mary Kerr, a girl from his home state of Pennsylvania. She was not his first choice. Years earlier, he had fallen in love with Elizabeth Brown, daughter of John Brown, the first pastor of Timber Ridge Church. She eventually rejected him, primarily because her mother disliked Graham intensely. Now that two centuries have passed I wish I could ask Mrs. Brown: "William Graham's name is writ in large letters across the face of Washington and Lee University. His impact and his influence are recognized all over America's intellectual climate. Has your opinion changed?"

Elizabeth must have been a remarkably attractive young lady. The next man to fall desperately in love with her was Oxford's new pastor, Samuel Eusebius McCorkle. From the historic journal of Philip Vickers Fithian, we know that young McCorkle had high hopes of claiming Elizabeth as his bride. His ardent efforts resulted in nothing more than total failure and heartbreak. In despair, our early pastor left Oxford for North Carolina where on July 2, 1776, he married Margaret Steele. They had ten children. McCorkle set up an academy where young students could prepare for college. When North Carolina State University at Chapel Hill celebrated its first graduating class of seven scholars, six of them had come from McCorkle's academy. Heartache had apparently made him stronger.

Who did the beautiful Elizabeth finally choose to marry? Not a preacher, quite, but the son of Rev. Alexander Craighead. His name was Thomas. An interesting note of history is that Rev. Craighead owned the hilltop where my new home "Magdalena" stands in 2007. I am the third Oxford pastor to occupy the site. When Craighead preached, Oxford folk had to go over to Whistle Creek, because there was no meeting house on Buffalo at the time. The second pastor involved was A.B. Davidson, whose home stood at the foot of today's Thorn Hill. Tom and Elizabeth's story fades out of sight. Hopefully they had a happy life together. Surely she had nights when she remembered how she had so disrupted the passion of two Oxford preachers.

The next of your early pastors to be disappointed in love was Daniel Blain. He fell in love with the pretty little redhead named Mary Moore, famous for her survival through incredibly cruel Indian captivity. By 1798, Mary had grown up. Her uncle had taken her in upon her return from the Ohio country. He lived near Natural Bridge, but Mary had other relatives at Timber Ridge and visited them often. Mary responded to Daniel Blain's energetic style, and she agreed to be his wife. A wedding was planned. It would take place at Falling Spring Meeting House, which along with Oxford, fell under the young theologian's charge.

Somehow things went wrong for Blain. His fiancé abruptly married another minister, the Reverend Samuel Brown, who was nearly a decade older than either Mary or Daniel. We are told that a woman has the right to change her mind. Mary exercised that right. Sam and Mary moved over to New Providence and built a lovely home that stands to the present day. Sam served as pastor of the church for the remainder of his life. It was a happy marriage. The couple produced at least twelve Presbyterian pastors in two generations. When Samuel died, his son-in-law took over the pulpit at New Providence Church.

Daniel Blain did not move away. Within seven months he was wed to Polly Hanna, to the relief of the Oxford people. They had suffered with their young pastor in his humiliation, heartbreak, and embarrassment. Now the jokes and snickers and gossip would end. For fourteen years Blain filled the pulpits of Oxford and Timber Ridge Churches. He and Polly lived in Lexington, midway between the two charges. He was a remarkably industrious clergyman, caring for two churches plus holding a position of full professor at the college, then called "Liberty Hall." In addition, he and some partners produced and published the sixty-four page *Virginia Religious Magazine* each month. Under Blain's leadership, Oxford built its first real church, the stone chapel that stood on the spot where our congregation now meets. The church interior looked different back in 1811. Pews were big wooden boxes, with doors closed during worship. The people could not see each other, but they could see the preacher high up near the ceiling under his sounding board. It seems to have been a good time for the church and the pastor, but the workload must have taken a toll. Blain died in 1814 at the age of forty-one—the only pastor to die in Oxford's service. He left Polly with six small children. Fifty years later one of his grandsons became pastor of the Collierstown Presbyterian Church.

Could Oxford properly be named "Heartbreak Hill?" Those dedicated young preachers did not enjoy much success with Timber Ridge girls. However, nearly two centuries later, Charles Bolivar Leech (Charlie Boy) went from Oxford over to Timber Ridge and won the heart of Mary Mackey Williams, whose ancestors were the first settlers. I find it satisfying to believe their marriage helped settle some scores and heal some scars.

Lesson 13:
Cabbages and Corn

The time has come, the walrus said,
To talk of many things:
Of ships and shoes and sealing wax,
Of cabbages and kings.

> — Lewis Carroll,
> *Through the Looking Glass*,
> 1871, McMillan, London

I love that verse because of the surprising incongruity between cabbages and kings. Rarely are both mentioned in the same conversation. Yet two of the common foods in early America can easily compete with kings. The time has come to talk of cabbages and corn.

German settlers in the Valley of Virginia, which was then the frontier, made a wonderful discovery. They could preserve fresh cabbage indefinitely simply by adding salt and water. The resulting mixture was called sauerkraut. It had miraculous qualities. Sauerkraut could not only keep you from starving, it could keep you healthy. Sailors all over the world had been dealing with a devastating illness brought on by nutritional deficiency. It was called scurvy and could be expected to appear on every long voyage. The new cabbage mixture held magic that prevented scurvy. This was a breakthrough of worldwide proportion. The lowly cabbage, fermenting in barrels, provided a simple, comprehensive solution to the ancient curse. Cabbages and kings suddenly became equally important.

Corn may claim even more importance than cabbages or kings. Without corn there would have been no American civilization. Natives of both South America and North America had cultivated corn hundreds of years before the coming of the white man. Our own ancestors had never heard of the wonderful grain. Yet on the frontier corn was the single crop that marked the line between survival and death. Early Jamestown settlers learned from the natives how to grow it in relative abundance. Still, in the early 1600s laws had to be passed requiring the white people to grow corn. They preferred to plant tobacco, which could produce more income per acre than any other crop. Although tobacco to this day remains a high-income product, it won't keep you alive. Corn will. It seems insane that the New World settlers would choose cash over survival, but it took the force of law to help common sense prevail.

The English word "corn" included all small grains. In our King James Bible, wheat is referred to as corn. Maize, which was unknown in the Old World, was obviously a grain, so the settlers called it corn. Today in America the word corn is used exclusively for maize. Corn is a unique plant. Unlike other vegetation, it has no cousins. We tend to take corn for granted, surrounded as we are with abundant acres of it. Yet upon closer examination, this food awakens our respect.

In the first place, corn is durable. I hold in my hand a yellow ear of corn as perfect as when I picked it last year. Without any preservatives, no refrigeration, and no special care, this food took care of itself in my garage. The shelf life of corn is almost infinite.

Corn is self-pollinating. The tiny embryonic kernels are fragile at first, so they wrap themselves in a tough interwoven husk. However, this isolates them from the necessary pollen. No problem. Every kernel sends a tiny silk line to the outside world, where pollen is falling from the tassel atop the stalk. The pollen is telegraphed back into the tight bundle, fertilizing one grain at a time. At maturity, the husk loosens just enough to allow air circulation for curing and hardening, all without assistance. Small wonder that the Native Americans considered maize sacred. In every Indian dialect the word for corn translates to mean "Our Life."

For the settlers, corn was a life-supporting miracle. The tough ear could be left hanging on the stalk all winter if desired, well above the snow level, preserving itself through all kinds of weather. When picked, the grain could be used as food with or without any preparation. In our valley it was ordinarily crushed and turned into meal. When a child asked for bread, he meant cornbread. Oxford frontiersmen made batter bread, ash cake, egg bread, hoe cake, corn dodgers, crackling bread, spoon bread, and corn pone…all from cornmeal. Then they made hush puppies, grits, corn pudding, corn syrup, and numerous desserts…all from the indestructible grain. At times folks were forced to resort to chestnut meal and acorn meal, but corn was their basic bread food.

Corn does not require processing. I can put this ear of corn in my hunting jacket. When hunger arises I simply shell off a handful of grain and eat it. The rock-like kernels do require some slow chewing, but the taste is rewarding, especially deep in the forest. If I don't eat it all in one season, the ear can rest in my pocket for several years and still be good to eat.

Corn is a prolific and dependable plant. Insert a single kernel into the soil, and with very little care it will produce two thousand of its kind. A single stalk may bear two and three ears. Today, just one acre, depending on the richness of the soil and sufficient rainfall, can bring forth three hundred bushels, far surpassing the yield of the frontier farm. Some varieties send their roots more than six feet into the earth, making them highly fruitful even during severe drought.

All of these unusual qualities cause me to view corn as a miracle. Today's media would have us believe that it will replace petroleum as an automobile fuel. I believe corn will always prove more valuable as food, for both man and beast, than as fuel.

Our Hebrew ancestors were sustained in the wilderness by a mysterious food called "*manna.*" In translation the word means, "What is it?" Wonderful as it was, manna would not keep. It had to be gathered daily, and it spoiled quickly. If you are offered a choice of manna or corn, choose corn every time. It is more of a miracle than manna.

Lesson 14:
Little Mary Moore: A True Survivor

James Moore and his wife Martha Poague thought they were making the correct decision when they packed their possessions and moved out of Rockbridge in 1775. At the time, James and Martha had four children. After settling in Abb's Valley near what is now Tazewell, the couple had five more children. The first of those was Mary, who developed into an unusually pretty girl with striking auburn hair.

Life went well for nine years. The valley was beautiful. The land was fertile. A ten-foot waterfall made constant music behind their sturdy log home. James Moore was a patriot who had served as an officer in the Revolutionary War. Now he prospered as a very successful farmer and father of a happy family.

However, in the autumn of 1784, James' fifteen-year-old son James Jr. suddenly disappeared. The few neighbors in the region joined the frantic search. Seeing moccasin tracks merging with the boy's footprints, it was soon realized that James Jr. had been killed or captured by Indians. Until this time there had been no evidence of danger from the red man. Little did the Moore family realize the horror yet to come.

A year passed without incident. Then in June of 1786, it happened. A band of Indians swooped down upon the home, killing the father and three children. Six people were taken captive— the mother Martha, her baby Margaret, her daughters Jane and Mary, her little son John, and a visiting girl named Martha Evans. All were hustled into the surrounding forest, beginning a forced flight that for Mary Moore and Martha Evans would encompass hundreds upon hundreds of painful miles. Poor little John, too small to keep up the fearful pace, was clubbed to death on the second day. Mary was forced to endure the sight of his scalp hanging from the belt of the exuberant murderer, day after day. A few days later, baby Margaret, crying from pain and exposure, was snatched from her mother's arms and smashed against an oak. The tiny corpse was scornfully draped over Mary's shoulders for some miles and then flung into forest undergrowth.

Could conditions be more horrible? Yes. Weeks later we find our nine-year-old heroine Mary with a stick, burying the charred bones of her mother and her sister Jane, who had been tied to a tree and burned alive. Mary Moore and Martha Evans survived through cold and hunger and unbelievable cruelty as they trudged through snow all the weary way to Canada. There they lived with their captors for a year or more, until Mary was sold as a slave to a cruel Canadian. Somehow she stayed alive, barely. Then a miracle finally happened.

Mary's brother James, lost three years earlier, reappeared in Canada. The strong young man had won the respect of his captors and had been freed. Although James had learned to live contently as an Indian, he was determined to bring his eleven-year-old sister home. With the untiring help of Thomas Evans, father of Martha, the two girls finally walked back. It took another year, making Mary Moore twelve years old when she was reunited with relatives here in Rockbridge. She grew to adulthood with her uncle Joseph Walker at Fancy Hill. They were active in Falling Spring Church.

Oxford's pastor, Daniel Blain, fell in love with Mary Moore, and they became engaged to be married. However, Mary suddenly changed her mind and in the autumn of 1798 married another preacher, Rev. Samuel Brown, of Timber Ridge and New Providence Churches. From all accounts Mary had made a good move. The marriage was happy, and her husband enjoyed material success. They built a beautiful, large brick home, Bellevue, in scenic Hays Creek Valley where they lived out their lives surrounded by an extraordinarily loving congregation of appreciative Presbyterians. They also ran a classical school in their home.

When Rev. Brown died, Mary kept the family of nine children together at Bellevue. Five of her sons became distinguished pastors, as did twelve of her grandsons and great-grandsons. Seventeen clergymen from one family! Twelve of the girls in that same generation married pastors. Almost all were Presbyterians, bringing the total to twenty-nine clergymen. The school in Bellevue produced an amazing array of scholars and statesmen, including James McDowell, Governor of Virginia, and Alexandra Gallatin McNutt, Governor of Mississippi. Mary's oldest daughter Frances married the new parson, James Morrison. He moved into Bellevue, kept the school functioning, and they added to the family with children of their own. Rev. Sam and James together served New Providence Church nearly sixty years.

Mary, who never topped one hundred pounds, suffered insomnia after her husband's death. She had a rocking bed built to fit her and thus gained relief. She never spoke of her childhood ordeal, but those horrors tormented her sleep. Mary's "cradle bed" is on display at the Rockbridge Historical Society building in Lexington. The amazing little lady with red hair left us quite a legacy. She and her husband rest in New Providence Cemetery just outside the church door.

Lesson 15:
The Hamilton School

Still sits the schoolhouse by the road,
A ragged beggar sleeping.
Around it still the sumac grows
And blackberry vines are creeping.

— J.G. Whittier,
In-School Days,
1875, Houghton Mifflin, New York

What we call the Hamilton School has the distinction of being the oldest of its kind yet standing. It was built as the result of a stirring religious revival, brought to Rockbridge by such illustrious pastors as William Graham, George Baxter, and Archibald Alexander.

In 1816, inspired by that revival, Rockbridge native Robert Hamilton decided to make a lasting contribution to the cause of Christ. An industrious and resourceful planter, Robert viewed hard work as essential to prosperity. But he also knew how to have a good time. This was an unusual trait among Scot-Irish Presbyterian settlers. "Uncle Bob," as he was called, would befriend anybody willing to hunt and fish. His home was known far and wide as a free hunting lodge. Some who came never left. Nobody would have called Robert Hamilton a religious man. But with the encouragement of Oxford's pastor, Rev. A.B. Davidson, the Hamilton family built a church. By 1823 it was erected and in use, on acreage donated by the Hamiltons. The deed specifically states: "It is a house of public worship. When not occupied for religious worship, the building may be used as a school. It is to be free for all preachers of the gospel, the oldest appointment to hold the preferences."

The log structure was a beehive of activity. Itinerant preachers, mostly Baptists and Methodists, were delighted with the sturdy facility. From the plain, homemade pulpit, they preached messages that were more fiery and appealing than the dignified eloquence of highly educated Presbyterian pastors. One young Rockbridge County native, William Taylor, began his ministry in that log church on Buffalo Creek. Taylor rose in the ranks of the Methodist Church to become Bishop of Africa. He preached on every continent of the world. Historians claim that Rev. Taylor "preached more widely than any member of the Christian Church in any age." Born on Hogback Mountain, this remarkable man was part of our Buffalo community before he moved into the position of "Bishop to the World," as he was called.

Another noted pastor to stand in that modest pulpit was the Reverend Samuel Houston. From his home near Natural Bridge, Rev. Houston would ride his horse across the steep Short Hill Mountain to perform marriages in Hamilton Church and to preach at Oxford. The aging pastor was related to Mrs. Robert (Sally) Hamilton and, through marriage, to the Hall family residing on its farm adjacent to Oxford Church.

Although Carmichael's famous 1883 map of Rockbridge shows Hamilton's as a church, the building was known more widely as a school. Robert and Sally Hamilton's children were educated there. Their daughter Nacissa began her teaching career there, later becoming one of the foremost women in the field of education in Virginia. John William Johnston, a member of our congregation

Hamilton School House in 2008

today, can be proud that his own mother Lora Shafer, who became Mrs. Granville Johnston, was educated in Hamilton School. She too returned to the school as teacher and was serving in that capacity when it finally closed in 1928. Students then went to Palmer Academy, four miles farther down the stream.

The old logs of Hamilton School speak of two centuries of history. The same sparkling trout stream makes music in the scenic cove. Many old graves dimple the lawn, the final resting place of local residents whose identities remain unknown, for no stones are engraved. It was here that Capt. John T. Wilson and Richard Manspile drilled their militiamen of Company H 8th Regiment in the early days of the Civil War. Hamilton's became the setting for boisterous political rallies marked by a generous supply of whiskey and by speeches so fiery that tempers flared and blood flowed from broken noses.

"Uncle Bob" Hamilton loved such amusements. He and his cronies were famous for wearing coonskin caps to the public events. The little log church was nicknamed "Coonskin College." Old photographs show that the solid plank front door was the community bulletin board.

After an outbreak of typhoid fever took the life of his son and several of his slaves, "Uncle Bob" sold off his extensive holdings and moved to Missouri in 1858, where he spent his remaining years. The Buffalo community mourned the departure of their colorful, successful, fun-loving citizen. Later, they mourned his death.

It is Narcissa who set the stone obelisk in Oxford's churchyard to commemorate her family. Although her father was buried in Missouri, this lasting monument to Uncle Bob stands just a few miles up the stream he loved to fish. Today we call it "Hamilton School."

Lesson 16:
James Waddell: The Blind Preacher

James Waddell, born in Ireland in 1739, came to America that same year in his mother's arms. Her influence gradually led little James into exceptional piety and into the Presbyterian ministry. But James Waddell was always a man in full. The notable historian William Henry Foote calls him a "man for all generations," a title given only to James Waddell.

As a teenager, young Jimmy had his hand severed by an accidental blow from his brother's axe during an exciting rabbit hunt. Although it was sewn carefully back together by his parents, the mutilated hand never functioned normally. Through the years and into adulthood, James longed for the touch of Jesus, who in that graphic story from the gospel healed the man with the withered hand. James moved from Pennsylvania to Virginia in pursuit of his theological education, and Virginia was his home for the remainder of his life. In 1762, he began his ministry in the Northern Neck, that low country where the great Potomac and Rappahannock Rivers enter the bay. Frail health drove him closer to the exhilarating climate we enjoy so casually. Rev. Waddell settled at Tinkling Spring Church near what is now the front entrance of Augusta Medical Center, just off Interstate 64.

During the Revolutionary War, Rev. James Waddell preached to our Rockbridge soldiers, one of whom was Samuel Houston, at Steeles Tavern on their way to defeat the British in the pivotal battle of Guilford Court House. History suggests that George Washington could have made use of such inspiring preaching when his army was suffering defeat after defeat in those earlier years of the war.

William Wirt in *Letters of a British Spy* gives us the most famous description of Waddell when total blindness had come upon him. Wirt had stopped by the meeting house not out of piety but curiosity. The first impression was dramatic:

Little did I suppose that in the wild woods of America I was to meet with a man whose eloquence would give to the sacrament a sublime pathos I had never before witnessed. As this blind old man descended from the pulpit to distribute the mystic symbols, there was more than a human solemnity in his manner, which made me shiver. He drew a picture of the suffering of Christ, the trial, the crucifixion and death. Although familiar, it was as if I was hearing the story for the first time. We hung on every word. The preacher, tears streaming, breathed the gentle prayer Christ uttered, "Father, forgive them, they know not what they do." The force of his feelings burst into an irrepressible flood of grief. The whole house resounded into the groans and sobs of the congregation. Raising his sightless eyeballs to heaven, clasping his hands to his breast, the tremulous old voice spoke in quiet fervor, "Socrates died like a philosopher, but Jesus Christ, like a God!" If the preacher had been an angel from heaven, the effect could scarcely have been more divine.

William Wirt could not forget the holy experience as he rode to Richmond. He felt that Waddell was the most stimulating orator in the world. He was astounded to find no one there who knew James Waddell, asking, "Is it not strange, that such a genius as this, so accomplished a scholar, so divine an orator, should be permitted to languish and die in obscurity, within 80 miles of the metropolis of Virginia?"

Today I can respond with some satisfaction: "Mr. Wirt, sir, here at Oxford, we would probably never have heard of you, had you failed to write of Rev. James Waddell. Is that not also strange?"

The saintly parson Waddell had to deal with more than a crippled limb and sightless eyes. Toward the end of his life, he was called before Presbytery to answer two charges: (1) He allowed his daughters to learn the formal dance called the minuet; and (2) He missed several Presbytery meetings. After a year of grueling procedures and endless testimony, the case was finally settled in favor of the frail old minister, which in my opinion says something good about Hanover Presbytery in 1796 and something bad about nitpicking hypocrites of any age. His daughter Janetta married a Rockbridge boy who was destined to become famous. Her husband's name: Reverend Archibald Alexander, founder of Princeton Theological Seminary.

Lesson 17:
Archibald Alexander: He Started Here

When studying the life of Archibald Alexander, I felt a surprising kinship stirring. He and I were both born in Rockbridge at Cornwall, which is a village two miles up from Mountain View School. Both of us received our formal education at what is now Washington and Lee University. Both of us spent lonely hours on Brushy Hill in prayer. We both became Presbyterian clergymen. And there the similarity ends. Archibald went on to fame. He had several advantages. He was born more than a century-and-a-half

Archibald Alexander

earlier than I, and he had William Graham as teacher.

Archibald's father William and Uncle Robert came from Ireland to America in 1737. From Pennsylvania they migrated into the Valley of Virginia and helped settle the huge grants of both Beverley and Borden. Archibald was born in 1771, on the opposite side of the valley from Oxford, a distance of approximately ten miles at the mouth of Irish Creek. His family assisted in the building of Timber Ridge Church, but none of them were pastors. Archibald changed that. He entered the ministry himself. Of his six sons, three became Presbyterian ministers; two were lawyers, and one was a physician.

Oxford has several intriguing connections with Archibald Alexander. His mentor was the brilliant William Graham, Oxford's pastor from 1788 to 1793. Archibald preached only twice in Rockbridge. One of those events happened here at Oxford Meeting

House. That boy from Cornwall began his ministry here where two hundred years later another lad from Cornwall (myself) is ending his. Little Archibald's friends called him "Lord Pigtail" because of the way he wore his hair. Generations later when I came along, the children from that same neighborhood called me "Horsetail." (Many of them never learned to say my name correctly, Horace Dale.) So there is one more similarity between us: "Pigtail" and "Horsetail."

Although always small and shy, Archibald forced himself to learn to speak eloquently and clearly. Long after he was ordained to the ministry, his reputation spread as being the amazing "boy preacher." By age twenty-five Archibald Alexander was president of Hampden Sydney College. His energy, intellect, and wise management turned the struggling school around, setting it on a course to become a leading college of the South. During this period he married Janette Waddell, beautiful daughter of the famous blind preacher. By all accounts, their marriage was extraordinarily blessed. She had every virtue of a good woman, wife, and mother. Janette's health never failed, and her notable affection for her distinguished husband never slackened in their long life together.

Archibald's college duties allowed time for extensive travel. He spent weeks and months touring the eastern half of America, preaching everywhere, and building enduring friendships with the leaders of our young nation. Archibald had a gift for remembering everything and everybody. Even in his seventies he could name every pastor and church in the entire Presbyterian denomination. His children grew up recalling how their father poured information upon them. He identified every plant to be found in the countryside. He remembered mathematical formulae. He spoke of each stream and valley and hilltop by name. He could quote the Bible for hours. When New England church leaders inquired where he received such impressive training, he said "in the mountains of Virginia." He was referring to our mountains and Rockbridge County.

Archibald Alexander was called from Hampden Sydney to a large church in Philadelphia where he served with growing distinction. By 1811, at age forty, he resigned the pastorate to take on the last job of his life, the founding and operation of Princeton Theological Seminary. It became one of the strongest graduate schools in America, educating thousands of prominent clergy. Princeton Seminary, adjoining the campus of Princeton University, owes its birth and the first forty years of its life to the boy from Irish Creek.

Thus Archibald Alexander may have influenced the world more than any other native of Rockbridge. Interestingly, few local people know of him. Some fifty years ago the Rockbridge Historical Society had an historic highway marker placed at the confluence of Irish Creek and South River where he was born, but the sign washed out soon afterward. Sadly, it appears no one has the money or motivation to replace it.

Archibald died in October 1851 at the age of eighty. Sweet Janette followed him less than one year later. They lie in the graveyard at Princeton, surrounded by headstones naming a veritable Who's Who of American giants. Some of them are: John Witherspoon, the only clergyman to sign our Declaration of Independence; Jonathan Edwards, who converted thousands of tough pioneers with such sermons as *Sinners in the Hands of an Angry God*; Samuel Davies, who gave much of his life to the freedom of religion in our country. And Archibald Alexander, founder of Princeton Seminary. Be proud to speak his name...he got his start here in Rockbridge.

Lesson 18:
John Robinson: From Rags to Riches

Oxford Church was only four years old in 1762, when John Robinson came from Ireland. John knew how to make a living with his hands. By age seventeen he had acquired skill as a weaver. Totally on his own, he worked his way from the port of Philadelphia to our frontier, in what would later be Rockbridge County but was called the "back part of Virginia" in the 1760s. Stopping at Red House on the Great Path, John Robinson met the lovely hostess Magdalena, twice widowed after losing first husband John McDowell and second husband Benjamin Borden. Magdalena and her new husband John Bowyer took in the witty Irish weaver, beginning a close life-long friendship. When John and Magdalena Bowyer moved to Lexington and built their new mansion on Thorn Hill, the "Weaver's Cottage" was constructed for Robinson in the side yard. There he lived and worked, producing strong fabric for those who could afford something better than homespun clothing. The cottage stands to this day.

John Robinson was twenty-three years of age when the Revolutionary War began. His friend John Bowyer rose to the rank of General during the conflict and doubtless was influential in making Robinson a "soldier of Washington" as inscribed on Robinson's monument. Both soldiers survived and returned to Thorn Hill.

Robinson then made a risky gamble and won. He had saved money by thrifty living, alone. Now he had a government certificate soldier's pay, which most people considered worthless. But John Robinson bought up all the certificates he could, paying ten percent cash for their face value. When the government finally redeemed them, he emerged, a man of wealth.

So John Robinson, the illiterate young veteran, consulted with John Bowyer, the highly educated and distinguished landowner who controlled "Borden's Grant" via his marriage to the wealthy Magdalena. The consultation ended with Bowyer selling "Hart's Bottom" to Robinson at a price that seemed scandalously high to all the Rockbridge neighbors.

John Robinson kept buying until he owned eight hundred acres of the bottomland. He bought fifty-seven slaves and began operating what may have been the most impressive plantation in Rockbridge. Records show that his farming effort hardly paid its way. However, two facets of the operation proved enormously lucrative: horse-trading and whiskey-making. Robinson was so gifted with judging horses that he became known far and wide as "Jockey Robinson." His distillery produced the "finest rye whiskey ever seen in Rockbridge County."

Although our hero could not read and write, he was extremely committed to education at all levels. When the Ann Smith Academy, founded by Oxford pastor David Blain, was facing bankruptcy, Jockey Robinson produced a bankroll that saved the school. He

John Robinson monument on the campus of Washington and Lee University.

is perhaps most renowned for his support of what we know as Washington and Lee University. Later, when the General Assembly of Virginia authorized the establishment of a state university, Robinson made an astonishingly generous offer of support, with the provision that the university be located at Lexington. The trustees of Washington College joined in, promising to donate everything they held. The combined offer far surpassed all other bids throughout the state. It looked as if the University of Virginia would certainly settle at Lexington. But Thomas Jefferson favored Charlottesville. His one vote trumped every voice and every bid. The year was 1818.

Jockey Robinson's generosity did not go unnoticed. Ann Smith Academy elected him as a trustee. He was also quickly placed on the Board of Trustees of Washington College, an honor normally conferred upon scholars and statesmen. Our illiterate Irish weaver was pleased but did not attend the meetings. He continued to donate large sums to Lexington schools, especially the college. In 1824 Robinson was an invited guest at the laying of the cornerstone for the first building of the present colonnade, thanks to his generosity. He also donated a fifteen-year-old barrel of superior whiskey for the celebration. Thirsty citizens by the hundreds made a rush on the open barrel. A riot took place, much to the embarrassment of Robinson and the distinguished orators. A semblance of order was restored only by deliberately upsetting the barrel and committing its costly contents to the sod.

Having no family ties, Robinson willed his entire estate to Washington College. It would be valued at millions in twenty-first century dollars. The college sold Hart's Bottom, all eight hundred acres. We don't call it a "bottom" any more. We call it the "City of Buena Vista, Virginia."

John Robinson died in 1826. He is buried in front of Robinson Hall on the Washington and Lee University campus. An impressive monument marks his grave. Take your children and show them. Tell them about a solitary young man from Ireland who worked his way from rags to riches. Although uneducated himself, he gave everything he owned to make certain that the blessing of education could be provided for others.

Lesson 19:
Snakefoot Territory

For more than one-and-a-half centuries, the narrow valley between Short Hill and Camp Mountain has borne the name "Snakefoot." Today if your mailing address includes South Buffalo Road or if your private lane fronts on that road, you may be surprised to learn that you reside in Snakefoot, Virginia.

From 1800 to 1857 one of the most colorful characters ever known in Rockbridge was making a name for himself a few miles upstream from Oxford Church. He was Robert Hamilton, the affluent donor of Hamilton Church, later called Hamilton School, which still stands on land he also provided. This man was distinguished in a number of ways. He was small in size but possessed a piercing wit and a generous heart. The entire community affectionately called him "Uncle Bob." Elite Lexingtonians, including the mayor, discovered that a visit to Bob's home was always rewarding. They enjoyed the country club atmosphere, the hunting, the fishing, the humorous stories, and the home-brewed whiskey provided at the fireside of this genial host.

Two of the Lexington sports, Alex Caruthers and the famous Col. Preston, had returned from an extended tour of the western United States where they had encountered some troublesome Snakefoot Indians. It was around 1835. Back in Rockbridge, Caruthers was visiting Uncle Bob Hamilton, and they were enjoying a leisurely horseback ride along Buffalo Creek. Bob's keen hunting eye was drawn to some tracks in the sand. They were human footprints left there by Elisha, a young neighbor. Bob was aware that the men of that family were tall and lanky, with amazingly long, slender feet. But as Caruthers dismounted and examined the barefoot impressions closely, he authoritatively declared, "Uncle Bob, these are none other than the tracks of a Snakefoot Indian. I've seen them out west, and I know what I'm seeing now."

Instead of correcting young Alex Caruthers, Bob demonstrated his personable fun-loving wit by responding, "You are absolutely correct. We are definitely in Snakefoot country!" Caruthers couldn't wait to get back to town and spread the news of his discovery. Enough people swallowed the story to make the name stick.

Judge Robert Johnston was born near Hamilton School. He became a member of the Confederate Congress. Despite his honorable status, Judge Johnston was commonly called "Snakefoot Johnston" in the polished halls of justice.

I searched the internet and found that there is a "Snakefoot Home School" in Rockbridge. Although unable to get more precise information, it is clear that the name has descended from Uncle Bob Hamilton and his frolics on South Buffalo Creek. "Snakefoot Lane" is a public road only a few miles uphill from Hamilton's home. I like to believe Uncle Bob still smiles each time someone writes that address. We do well to remember Robert Hamilton and to speak his name. He is a good role model for us and for our children. The same can be said for Uncle Bob's daughter Narcissa, who faithfully maintained the home after her mother Sally, Uncle Bob's wife, died at age thirty-nine. The noble Hamilton family overcame grief and sadness. Their home continued to radiate glowing hospitality for another quarter century. In the late 1850s they moved to Missouri. But Snakefoot Territory remains on Buffalo. The Hamilton plot is clearly marked in Oxford's graveyard. Hamilton's log school/church stands guard beside the ancient stream. Fortunate newcomers, old and young, still laugh and live with the radiant legends and the comforting heritage of the Clan of Hamilton.

LESSON 20:
Sam Houston:
From Timber Ridge to Texas

To be born in a churchyard must be a good thing. Little Sam Houston's family gave the land for the stone church at Timber Ridge in the 1750s. It stands to this day, one quarter of a millennium later, still in use. Sam was born April 2, 1793, in a house only a few feet from the church door. There he grew in body and mind, learning the skills necessary for frontier living. He swam and fished in Mill Creek below the house. With rifle and axe he roamed the same hills that surrounded my own childhood home, although I came along much later. Sam's father was a military man and obviously taught the lad how to win wars. After the death of his father, Sam and his mother moved to Tennessee. As they said goodbye, an uncle said, "I have little hope for Sam. He is so wild." The boy quickly responded, "Uncle, some day I will come back through here on my way to Congress." He did just that, several times.

On the frontiers of Tennessee, Sam enlisted as a soldier. His size and strength were legendary. In battle he was ferocious and methodical. He was elected to Congress and served with such popularity that in a few years was elected governor of Tennessee. Then Sam took a wife, and suddenly things went bad. On his wedding night the tearful bride blurted out an awful truth: she was in love with another and only married Sam because her parents insisted on her becoming the governor's wife. The lights went out in the governor's mansion. They also went out in our hero's heart. Mounting his horse, the gallant governor rode off without a backward glance and went to live with the Indians. The crisis at the capitol would be handled by lesser politicians. Sam was not coming back.

The red men loved Sam Houston. The chief of the Cherokees adopted as a son this big white man from Rockbridge and named him "The Raven." Sam Houston won universal respect among all

American Indians and eventually became their advocate in the U. S. Congress. Federal lawmakers were impressed. Here, finally, was a man of valor who knew how to deal with Indians. Congress sent Sam to Texas to make treaties with border tribes so that trading and commerce could flourish. In the years that followed, not a single treaty was broken, proving that Sam Houston knew what he was doing.

By 1835 Houston had become commander-in-chief of the armies of Texas during the war with Mexico. It was Gen. Sam Houston who clearly saw how the Alamo was a death trap for Americans and ordered its evacuation. His order was ignored, resulting in the shocking death of every man there, including Davy Crockett. But the Mexican triumph under Santa Anna was short lived. Sam Houston, with seven hundred soldiers, caught up with Santa Anna's 1,800 and simply wiped out the Mexican army, losing only thirty-one of his own. The victory there at San Jacinto established the independence of the Republic of Texas, with Sam Houston as its first and only president. When Texas became a state, he became first a senator and then governor of Texas. However, Sam's life as a governor failed again. The year was 1861. Texas wanted to secede and join the Confederacy. Sam Houston flatly refused, believing that Civil War in America was lunacy. Once again the tall man moved out of a governor's mansion.

Gen. Houston had married again, and this time it worked. He had four sons and four daughters. Although Sam Houston had never been a good student, preferring guns over books, his children distinguished themselves as scholars. Their dad was famous. To this day, April 21 is a Texas holiday (every year since 1836) commemorating Houston's decisive victory at San Jacinto. Portraits of Sam Houston are displayed like flags in every chamber of government, and a full size statue stands in Austin. Houston, Texas, is named for the boy from Rockbridge.

What is General Sam Houston's connection with Oxford? His aunt Esther (Mrs. James McKee) is buried in our graveyard.

His cousin, the Reverend Samuel Houston, was pastor here. Some members of our current congregation are relatives. We are breathing the same Valley air that made Sam Houston a great man. Your own parents and grandparents understand the vanishing traits that were instilled in young Sam. A Scottish verse sums it up:

> *They raised them rough, they raised them well.*
>
> *If their feet were pointed in the paths of hell*
>
> *They put in their souls the fear of God*
>
> *And tanned their hides with a stiff ramrod.*

Monument marking birthplace of Sam Houston at Timber Ridge, placed there by state of Texas.

Lesson 21:
Big Foot Wallace

I f you have never heard of Big Foot Wallace, there was a time when Mexico would have envied you. Those people had heard too much of him. Wallace and another Rockbridge County boy named Sam Houston were making things difficult in Mexico and were altering the course of the country's history.

"Big Foot" was born in 1817 on the family farm a mile or so to the southeast of Lexington, Virginia. His full name is William Alexander Anderson Wallace. He inherited good genetics through such remarkable forebears as the lady Magdalena (frequently cited in these history lessons) and his noble grandfather Samuel Wallace. The first court of Rockbridge County was held at the Wallace home in 1789. Thirty years later William arrived. He grew strong and unusually tall. His spirit was fearless and cheerful. The blood of bold patriots flowed in his veins, and William was aware of it. Rockbridge people knew and recounted the exploits of gallant Wallace heroes.

When William was twenty years old, his brother Samuel died at the hands of Mexicans in what some refer to as the massacre of Goliad, Texas. William's fighting spirit was ignited. He vowed vengeance upon Mexico. That vow set the course for his life. With two comrades, James Paxton and Franklin Shields, they left Rockbridge and set off for Texas. The record tells us that they headed due west from Lexington, taking the route through Collierstown and over the mountains. In Texas, William became a soldier in John Hays' ranger squad, where he quickly won admiration as an uncommonly gifted warrior. In several historic battles, William made Mexicans pay dearly for his brother's death. Vengeance was extracted through the unerring marksmanship of Wallace's famed rifle.

He was not always on the winning side. In 1842 he was captured and spent sixteen miserable months in a Mexican prison. During that period a charitable group of Americans donated shoes for the confined soldiers, but nothing would fit William's feet. Eventually a pair was locally crafted in a size large enough for him. From that day onward, he was known as Big Foot Wallace.

After the Mexican War, William became a "Pony Express Rider." He may be the only native of Rockbridge to win that title. He would cover five hundred miles a week on horseback. Through storm and danger he never failed to deliver the mail from San Antonio to El Paso. There were times when he was forced to use his guns with deadly accuracy. Eventually the robbers and the Indians learned to back off from this lone rider who gave the appearance of vulnerability. Texans were so impressed with Big Foot's many contributions to their state that the legislature gave him nearly 1,300 acres on Galveston Island. Due partly to his own carefree attitude, Big Foot Wallace never gained free title to the land.

The *Lexington Gazette* of December 1933 sadly recounts that Big Foot's last years were marked by poverty and loneliness, despite his legendary heroism. William Wallace died in 1899 and was buried in San Antonio. Here in Rockbridge, some effort has been made toward preserving the memory of a native son. A Presbyterian pastor named E.W. McCorkle began a campaign to erect a marker in Lexington. When McCorkle was stricken with serious illness, M.W. Paxton, editor of the *Rockbridge County News*, took charge of the project and brought it to completion in 1936. A bronze plaque set in marble now stands at the corner of Main and Houston Streets in the town. The inscription is headed, "Big Foot Wallace: 1817–1899." The text announces his birth nearby and summarizes his life in Texas. It also affirms that Texas has "signally honored his memory" and that his ordeals are recorded in history.

We know that people in Texas honor Sam Houston, the Rockbridge neighbor of Big Foot. They were instrumental in placing a monument near Houston's birthplace at Timber Ridge Church. Texans named a major city for Houston, and his statue stands in their state capitol. The memory of Big Foot Wallace is not as bright, but perhaps this short account will help it to endure. As you drive north on Main Street into Lexington, you will pass Wallace Street, named in honor of Big Foot's family. The next main intersection at the Mayflower House is where his monument rests in the hedge, at the corner of Houston Street. Stop and salute this tall soldier, Pony Express Rider, and Indian fighter who in life was so admired and loved. The story of such a Rockbridge hero and his notable family must not be forgotten.

Big Foot Wallace Marker at the intersection of South Main and Houston Streets in Lexington.

Lesson 22:
Meeting House Lane

M ost of us have difficulty visualizing the Rockbridge area when there were few roads. During the first generation there was hardly a wheeled vehicle to be seen, not so much as a wooden cart. People mostly walked, following animal paths. If they were fortunate enough to have horses, the path would accommodate one animal at a time, in single file. A packhorse could carry an average load of two hundred pounds. If two poles with ends dragging were affixed to a willing horse, the load could be slightly increased. When they came, our pioneer forefathers brought very few possessions.

Roads were soon laid out to Williamsburg, and one already existed to Philadelphia. Great droves of cattle were driven out of the valley to Philadelphia markets from the 1730s onward. Most of the early paths have disappeared. Some of them evolved into highways. The Midland Trail became Rt. 60. The Great Path is now U.S. Rt. 11. One path that has withstood the ravages of time and nature is Meeting House Lane, although it too is rapidly fading from living memory. This lesson intends to preserve some of its history.

On the western edge of the Rockbridge frontier lies a series of fertile valleys drained by Buffalo Creek and its branches. By 1740 homesteads were appearing. Most of the people were Scot-Irish Presbyterians. They were serious about matters of faith but rejected the official state church, the Anglican Church of England. They were called "dissenters." To pursue their chosen religion, Buffalo Presbyterians would walk across the hills on Sunday to assemble at Hall's Meeting House on Whistle Creek. The trek required two hours of strenuous legwork each way. Old records indicate that this practice continued for nearly twenty years.

A change came about not because of distance but because of danger. The French and Indian War encouraged Native Americans to drive out all the white intruders. By 1760 it had become clear that if the settlers were to survive, they must have secure shelters designed for defense within every community. On the banks of Buffalo Creek, a sturdy log fort was built. The structure was large enough to accommodate all who lived nearby. The fort was quickly recognized as a logical place for meetings, whether for fighting or for worship. Until 1773 it bore the title of Upper Buffalo Meeting House. For reasons not recorded, the name was later changed to Oxford, a familiar classical title from the old country.

Oxford Meeting House was visited so regularly by itinerant preachers it became accepted as a primary place of worship. The paths of the Buffalo Creek community led to Oxford. One path became designated Meeting House Lane. It was heavily used by the settlers living along the mountain boundary to the west in an area later known as Collierstown. For an astonishing ninety years, Meeting House Lane brought more souls to Oxford than all the other paths combined.

More roads eventually developed and brought changes. The Lexington-Covington Turnpike was completed in 1832, connecting the Valley of Virginia with settlements far to the west. That major transportation route, wide enough to permit wheeled wagons, bypassed Oxford and passed through Collierstown. Rather suddenly commerce and population were drawn to the road. Rev. A.B. Davidson, pastor of Oxford, was enterprising enough to recognize a promising location. There at the foot of the mountain, before travelers begin the steep ascent westward, or after they have come down from the west, is a natural place to pause. The pastor and some of his flock built another meeting house. It occupied a scenic knoll atop a huge limestone formation jutting out into Colliers Creek. The visual impression is that of a ship entering the waterway. They named their place of worship Ship Rock Shed. A few years later it was expanded and given the name Ship Rock Meeting House.

A village arose here where the stagecoaches stopped. Commercial activity became self-generating. First came a tavern, then lodging and eating places. The village turned into a town, Collierstown, complete with town hall, Masonic lodge, the Cormorran Institute for young ladies, several mills, blacksmith shops, stores, and medical facilities. Historic data reflect more than thirty commercial establishments thriving along Colliers Creek by the mid 1800s.

By contrast, Oxford suffered neglect. Rev. Davidson continued to hold services there occasionally, but then moved the communion ware, the official records, and the session meetings to "New Oxford," as Ship Rock Meeting House came to be called. "Old Oxford" was abandoned. The flow on Meeting House Lane reversed direction. People on Buffalo, if they were to enjoy Sabbath observances, were now required to walk from Old Oxford to New Oxford. To this day historians are frustrated when they encounter the Oxford name. Which Oxford? There were two of them, slightly more than two miles apart. Certainty, however, is assured when the subject has to do with graveyards.

Pioneers in the 1760s brought a custom with them to Rockbridge from the Old World—the burial of their dead in the churchyard. On Buffalo, that meant Old Oxford. Around the log fort, the community graveyard spread. Most of the graves were unmarked or marked with wooden markers that have rotted away over the years. When the stone church was built nearby, the cemetery expanded. Even during the years when the church was closed, the burials continued. Old Oxford held a monopoly. People could be persuaded to walk over the hill to New Oxford for Sunday services, but they insisted on being laid to rest near their loved ones.

In the winter of 1851–52 James Dove died in Collierstown. Despite heavy snows, his friends scheduled a burial at the only community cemetery. The body was placed on a two-horse sled for the trip across Meeting House Lane. In those days it was the custom for the family of the deceased to provide a generous supply of whiskey for all mourners. Funerals were turned into party-time as people drowned their sorrow in adult beverages.

Old Presbytery documents bristle with stern rulings attempting to discourage the hilarity. Those rulings eventually prevailed, but not in time to help James Dove. On that winter day, bitter cold called for a cup of cheer. Grief demanded a second cup, or more. When all were assembled at the Oxford graveyard, they discovered that Mr. Dove was not present. He had rolled unnoticed from the sled. Billy Moody and his uncertain crew retraced their steps up Meeting House Lane and found the body lodged against a cedar tree. This time they succeeded and the funeral went forward.

In 1856, a brick church was built four hundred yards downstream from the Ship Rock. The name was changed to Collierstown Presbyterian Church, and it would have a cemetery. At the east end of Meeting House Lane stood the decrepit stone meeting house and its one-hundred-year-old graveyard. The people of Buffalo were determined to have a working church on the spot. The Presbytery finally approved the effort, recognizing it as a new church development. Stubborn farmers were also given permission to name their new church. In a display of great

Oxford Church as seen from Meeting House Lane in 2008.

common sense they announced to Presbytery, "the name of our new development shall be Old Oxford Presbyterian Church."

Paved roads now connect Oxford and Collierstown. They meander along the streams and follow gentler grades. The routes are admittedly more convenient, but they are less romantic than Meeting House Lane where first came buffalo, then Indians, then tough Presbyterians on their walk to church. From the pinnacle they had breathtaking views of the Blue Ridge to the east and the Alleghenies to the west, with lush valleys in between. Whether the sermon was inspiring or not, such scenery surely made Meeting House Lane a worthwhile hike on the Lord's Day.

Lesson 23:
We Shall Have a New Brick Church

It was time for Oxford Church to take a deep breath. The horror of the Civil had finally ended but was not forgotten. Six years earlier every person had been forced to make a decision: Am I for the Union, or am I for the Confederacy? There was no middle ground. Families split over the issue. Tempers flared. Barns were burned in the dead of night, because the owner chose a side. Oxford Church buried some of her finest young men fallen in battle. The year was 1866. The piercing pain of war still throbbed. Poverty and uncertainty bewildered Virginia.

With morale devastated, the economy in ruins, and a northern general overseeing occupied territory, how on earth could the little rural congregation decide to build a new church? Even in good times Presbyterians have trouble deciding anything, especially if it involves spending money. But Oxford Church people not only decided, they built. The entire process was an extraordinary accomplishment, proving that nothing is impossible for people of faith. The handsome sanctuary we meet in today stands as a tribute to their determination. Their purpose was threefold: to thank God for the ending of war; to honor the men who had fallen; and to provide a lasting temple of worship for their children's children. The story brings tears to our eyes.

Rev. John Andrew Scott shed the military chaplain's uniform to serve as Oxford's part-time pastor. His full-time job was with Ann Smith Academy in Lexington, where he was principal. Captain Scott was the right man at the right time for Oxford's pulpit. All of the returning veterans had great respect for the warrior-preacher. They were eager and willing to serve God under his leadership.

The sweet stone building had stood for a half-century. Now it was carefully and lovingly dismantled. All usable material was salvaged and saved. Bricks were fired at the site, from good clay found here in the churchyard. Most of the stone went back into the new foundation, some of which lay on the footprint of the old church. Money proved to be extremely scarce during those austere times. The little congregation soon realized that self-sacrifice was required in order for the church to be completed. Women rode buggies to Lexington, selling their baskets of butter and eggs. This time the money did not buy children's shoes. Instead, they donated it to a sacred cause. Men got together for collective butchering times and then peddled the meat from door to door in town, a few pounds at a time. They added the hard earned cash to the building fund.

Construction was slow and discouraging, but the craftsmanship was uncompromising. The people gave more than they could spare, because they were proud of what they were doing. They envisioned their church as the Biblical light upon a hill that would shine forth to the glory of God. We owe them something. They put us to shame.

After two years, it was time to set the roof in place. Nearby lay the pile of salvaged timbers. The contractor started splicing the old lumber for roof supports. He put a number of them in place, contrary to the strong advice of Granville Campbell, who considered them undependable. Campbell, a seasoned builder and an elder of Oxford, had made the bricks and knew about construction. His opinion should have been heeded. One of the old timbers broke, severely injuring the contractor and two other workers. The construction was eventually resumed but no more second-hand lumber was considered. The bad news for us is that here in our church some of those old beams arch above our heads today. The good news is that they have proven sound all these 140 years.

I must insert another note with regard to Granville Campbell. His son James, only a few years after the accident, was called to the ministry. James completed his college education and entered Union Theological Seminary, fully intending to become a Presbyterian pastor. While in seminary James suddenly fell ill and died, forcing Oxford Church to deal with one more tragedy.

Some years later Granville himself needed medical treatment in Baltimore. Leaving Oxford valley, the carriage was halted atop Kyger Hill. The noble man had a premonition. For long moments Granville Campbell gazed down at the dear church he had helped build. He cherished the bright Sabbath mornings in his memory, and the times he had gone there to meet his friends and to be close to his God. His soul drank in the glorious panorama of meadows and mountains. Slowly the carriage moved on. It was his final view, for Granville died in Baltimore. He and his wife Sarah now lie in the graveyard just outside our church's front door, surrounded by friends and fields they loved so much. I feel that I know them, but I wish I could have met them.

The new brick church was dedicated on August 8, 1869, after three painful years of construction. A Lexington newspaper printed this note:

> We congratulate the Oxford people upon the auspicious indications which attend the opening of their new house of worship. The Church is a very fine, substantial brick building sufficiently commodious to accommodate a much larger congregation than usually assembles there. Here is a fine opening for a young preacher who wishes to be useful. The Church is presently looking out for a pastor.
>
> — *Virginia Gazette*,
> Lexington, Virginia, August 11, 1869

Reverend Scott had moved on. A considerable debt continued to hang over the congregation, even after embarrassing appeals were published in local newspapers. The church pleaded for financial help from Presbytery and almost got it. But the request was finally denied. Why? Ironically, the church bureaucracy viewed our fertile valley as a virtual Garden of Eden, a land flowing with milk and honey. The people buckled down, rolled up their sleeves, and sacrificed some more. Nine years from the beginning of construction, the debt was finally eliminated.

The moral of this story: Nothing Oxford faces today can compare with the challenge of 1866. Our forebears did what needed to be done. So can this congregation. So can we all.

Oxford Church in 2008

Lesson 24:
Commerce on Buffalo

People who visit Lake Robertson for the first time think they have come to the most remote end of the world. They cannot imagine the thriving commerce that once flourished along the Colliers Creek branch of Buffalo.

In 1832 the Lexington-Covington Turnpike, laid off by the famous Claudius Crozet, was completed. That trail has always looked rough and steep and primitive, especially on North Mountain. However, the modest road through Collierstown served as a major east-west connection from Richmond to Charleston. All stagecoaches stopped at the foot of the mountain, regardless of destination.

There in Collierstown, tolls were collected, horses were changed, and travelers were fed. The inn also provided lodging and entertainment. Several blacksmith shops were kept busy, indicating a strong flow of traffic. There was a factory for making wagons. You could purchase a new firearm or hat or pair of boots, all manufactured in Collierstown. If eyeglasses were needed, you could go to the optical shop inside Morrison's store to be fitted for those. Trials were held in the Temperance Hall. Solemn assemblies took place in the Masonic Temple. Captain James Harper established an advanced school for young ladies called the Commoran Institute. Proud girls came from considerable distance to board in Collierstown and attend that school until it was succeeded by Marmion High School.

In 1902, G.P. Hutton wrote an article for the *Rockbridge County News* describing the area as he recalled it during the last half of the 1800s. In the few miles between Lake Robertson and what is now Effinger, Hutton lists more than thirty commercial establishments, including schools and churches. An example is "Marmion," located where the Potter-Wade mill still stands today. At Marmion there was a store, a barrel factory, a tannery, a post office, and the medical facility of Dr. W.P. Rogers, all in addition to the mill. A photograph of Marmion can be found on page eight of Carmen Clark's *History of Collierstown Presbyterian Church*.

I found that Carmichael's map of 1883 shows four large water-powered mills on Collier's Creek. Post offices were established at Alphin, Collierstown, Marmion, and Murat. It is small wonder that Rev. A.B. Davidson, pastor of Oxford, could envision Colliers Creek as the most promising area for church progress. He gradually turned his attention in that direction. Davidson moved the session meetings from Oxford to Collierstown, as well as the communion ware and the church records. Our stone church stood on this hill, abandoned. For nearly one hundred years Presbyterians from Collierstown had trekked across Meeting House Lane to worship here. Now it was all reversed. A log building called Ship Rock Meeting House was the new destination. Rev. Davidson began calling it New Oxford, much to the resentment of our ancestors. The preacher felt the sting, and attempted to make the separation complete by placing the Oxford area in a different Presbytery. Davidson urged that the boundary follow Colliers Creek, with everything on the south side to be part of Montgomery Presbytery. All churches on the north side of the creek, including Ship Rock, would remain in Lexington Presbytery. He almost succeeded. Boundaries were redrawn. Falling Spring Church and High Bridge Church were placed in the southern Presbytery, ending their close connection with Oxford. Our church, dead as it was, stayed in the old presbytery. There is some irony in history: a fine brick church replaced Ship Rock by 1856, but it was built on the south side, or wrong side, of Colliers Creek. Davidson had not forseen that possibility.

Another note of interest involves Granville Campbell, patriarch of Buffalo. He helped finance construction of "New Oxford" brick church in Collierstown. He rented one of the more expensive pews for his family. Only ten years later we find Granville spearheading the restoration of Old Oxford. He was largely responsible for building the edifice we are sitting in today. One wonders, did he get tired of Meeting House Lane or were more emotional issues involved? Be aware that the present one-mile scenic road between Oxford and Effinger was not there until the early 1900s. The old route followed Meeting House Lane to the crest of the hill behind Oxford and then branched north, descending to Agnor's Mill on Colliers Creek some quarter-mile above the mouth of Toad Run (Effinger).

The "Buffalo Side" was spared the intense development that the turnpike had brought to Collierstown. Nevertheless, mills and stores and post offices continued to operate over here as well. The big watercress operation lay almost in sight of Oxford Church. Palmer Academy appeared in the vale. Upstream was Oak Dale, Virginia, with its own post office. The Blue Grass Trail, only a few hundred yards from Oxford's front door, carried hopeful migrants into the promising meadows of Kentucky, following North Buffalo. South Buffalo was busy too, with Rapps Mill, Virginia, boasting its own post office, store, mills, onyx mine, tannery, and distilleries. Between Rapps and Oxford was another post office named Side Way, Virginia. Our church's address might have been Oak Dale or Side Way, but it fell to another post office across Kyger Hill. Oxford's mailing address was Murat, Virginia, until rural free delivery came in the 1920s, allowing mailboxes along all busy roadsides.

How did our post office acquire its unusual name of Murat (pronounced "mew-raw")? For many years the location was called Bolivar Mill, for the mill located a couple of miles upstream from Zollman, Virginia, at the eastern foot of Kyger Hill where Buffalo exits the gorge. During construction there was debate as to the best name for the Virginia post office. Many assumed it would keep the name of the mill and schoolhouse. Others wanted something more romantic.

Finally the post office was ready for business, but still unnamed. The exasperated postmaster declared, "The very next being to walk in this door will name our post office!" In walked a large tomcat. One man jokingly asked, "Okay, kitty, what is the name?" The cat, without hesitation, looked up and said plain as day, "Mew-raw." The postmaster accepted the name. He said, "I know about Murat. He is a famous French general. He served under Napoleon and sought refuge in America. It's a good name."

It must be. More than a hundred years later the name stands. Although the building has vanished, Murat Road remains. The dateline for a present-day local newspaper column reads "Murat." In the world's languages, c-a-t is not always pronounced "cat." R-a-t is not always pronounced "rat." Even a semi-literate country tomcat should understand that much French. Think of that cat when you say "Murat," and you'll get it right.

Murat Post Office

Lesson 25:
John Preston: He Met His Match

John Thomas Lewis Preston was accustomed to having his way. He was big, handsome, intelligent, highly educated, and wealthy. He grew up in an environment where people accepted the idea that the man of the house was without question the monarch and master. However, a small woman named Maggie Junkin brought about a change in John and in his world of nineteenth-century Lexington, Virginia.

Born here in 1811, the year in which a stone church replaced Oxford Meeting House, John had a privileged childhood. His parents sent him to a preparatory school in Richmond, where his close friend was Edgar Allen Poe. His quest for formal education brought him back to Lexington where he graduated from Washington College. John also completed postgraduate work at the University of Virginia and Yale before settling in his hometown as a lawyer.

John Preston married Sarah (Sally) Caruthers, and together they produced seven children. In 1856, during delivery of what would have been their eighth child, Sally and her newborn infant both died. Preston was distraught. He appears to have been very much in love with Sally, and on her tombstone he wrote fervent words of devotion. John sent his younger children to live with his sister, Elizabeth Cocke in Cumberland County. A few years later Elizabeth would provide a home for Gen. Robert E. Lee on the same farm following his surrender at Appomattox.

Severely depressed, John Preston turned for comfort to his friend Thomas Jackson, who had suffered the loss of his own wife Eleanor, who was Margaret Junkin's sister. Although Jackson was an instructor at VMI, he lived with his Junkin in-laws on the campus of Washington College. Margaret (Maggie) was living there also. Her keen intelligence and sharply honed mind allowed her to join in the evening conversations with her father

George Junkin, president of Washington College, and the two VMI professors, Preston and Jackson. Maggie described herself as an "old maid" at age thirty-seven, but she was not a retiring type of personality. She never took a back seat in any gathering of intellectuals. Maggie quickly became a source of consolation for John. She had been Sally's close friend. The grieving quartet bonded. Jackson and Maggie became so close they may have married, except that their Presbyterian religion outlawed it at the time because of their in-law relationship. There was no such restriction applying to Maggie's relationship with Major Preston.

John and Maggie fell in love. Dr. Junkin was delighted. He admired the wealthy, mature lawyer-turned-teacher. He urged his hesitant daughter to marry, insisting in his characteristic dictatorial style that "the very finger of God" was pointing her in that direction. She consented. But trouble arose immediately. Major Preston set the wedding date for next August 2, and Maggie absolutely rejected it. Why? Because it had been the date of John and Sally's wedding. Astonished at Maggie's insubordination, the "alpha male" asserted his superiority by storming, "You will marry me on that date or not at all!" Calmly little five-foot Maggie replied, "John, it has been nice knowing you. Goodbye." She walked away.

The big outdoorsman was dumbfounded. Maj. J.T.L. Preston, aristocrat, had met his match. He no doubt assumed that since August 2 had produced a happy first marriage, why not repeat it for the second, and have only one anniversary date to remember? Preston was a man in a man's world. He did not know it, but he was definitely in need of some "sensitivity training." Only through the desperate intervention of Jackson and Dr. Junkin did a compromise finally emerge. The date was reset for August 3. Maggie's father officiated. The groom was grim. He had lost the first fight.

By all accounts the marriage developed into a happy relationship. Henry Boley, writing eighty years later, says in his book *Lexington In Old Virginia*: "Doubtless the most distinguished couple ever to have lived in Lexington was Co. J.T.L. Preston and his talented wife Margaret Junkin." What made them so distinguished? She was the "poet laureate of the south," as I explain in a separate lesson. He claimed distinction in a multitude of achievements.

Of interest to Oxford is the fact that Preston visited the community and this church often as a guest of Bob Hamilton. He helped name Buffalo Valley "Snakefoot Territory." His prizewinning hounds could be heard sounding among our hills, coon hunting on long moonlit nights. In Lexington John Preston conceived, promoted, and named the Virginia Military Institute. He taught Latin there throughout the last half of his life. With Col. Francis Smith, Preston was in charge of the historic execution of John Brown at Harpers Ferry, and he wrote eloquently of the experience. He helped his friend Thomas Jackson establish and teach in the first-of-its-kind Sunday school for slaves.

As a colonel he commanded troops in the Civil War. His son Frank was captain of the cadets in the Battle of New Market in 1864. John Preston was chief protagonist and final victor in the "Skinner War" (the subject of another lesson in this book), in which a fiery Scottish parson of Lexington Presbyterian Church attempted to sue his own church elders. Col. Preston was also generous. When a fellow elder died poor, Preston had him buried in the Preston Plot

Preston Oak in the Stonewall Jackson Cemetery.

under a large stone engraved with "John B. Lyle, the truest friend, the bravest man, and the best Christian ever known." During and after the war, Preston taught at VMI without pay. Preston lived to see one of his sons rise to the position of pastor of the Lexington Presbyterian Church from 1883 to 1895.

Preston considered himself superior in the art of loving. He wrote, "That man who knows better than I do how to appreciate and return the love of a noble woman, I never expect to meet." His assessment of himself sounds strange to our ears, considering his lack of understanding about women's regard for their own wedding anniversary date. His wife Maggie had forgiven him for that shortcoming. She wrote unusually tender love poems about her feelings for John. There were moments however, when Maggie's patience was tested, as when he failed to return with his soldiers after a mission. She suffered awful apprehension for another full night and day, convinced that he was disabled or dead. Finally he showed up, explaining lamely, "Since we failed to find Yankees, I went deer hunting instead." So we have another clear case showing John's need for sensitivity training. He could have spared her needless suffering. She commented in her writings of his lack of empathy.

Col. Preston and his family are buried in the Stonewall Jackson Cemetery. They lie beneath a towering tree called the "Preston Oak." The old patriarch, dominant all his life, has had more than a hundred years to get reconciled to the odd fact that the massive tree is not named for him. In *Historic Trees of Virginia* it is listed as "The Margaret Junkin Preston Oak." In life, as in death, the little lady was a match for her powerful husband.

Read their moving epitaphs located near the front entrance of the graveyard:

John T.L. Preston,
officer of the commonwealth,
of the confederate states, and of the Church of Christ.
He finished his course. He kept the faith.

Sara Caruthers Preston:
she was the joy of her husband's heart
and the light of his household for more than 23 years.

Margaret J. Preston:
her song cheered the heart of the
southern people in the hour of their deepest distress.

Lesson 26:
Margaret Preston: Lexington's Songmaker

Lexington, Virginia, was a village of one thousand residents. The little town could not have realized the significance of the stagecoach arrival one December night in 1848. Heavy snowfall had disrupted all normal schedules. Dr. George Junkin and his family climbed from the coach at midnight. He was the new president of Washington College. Dr. Junkin had acquired a national reputation as an orator, teacher, and Presbyterian pastor. The greater influence of his auburn haired daughter Margaret, eventually eclipsed his fame.

M.J. Preston

"Little Maggie" was only five feet tall, but she was a powerhouse in both mind and body. Her father had carefully instructed his firstborn himself. She never became a professor, although she knew more about most subjects than any college instructor. She was fluent in Greek, Latin, French, and English. She understood science and higher mathematics. She had virtually memorized the Bible. Maggie's scholastic prowess, however, did not keep her indoors. She baffled Lexington women with her athletic hiking, miles at a stretch, night or day. Margaret was twenty-eight years old when she first saw Lexington's gaslights through the blinding snow. It was to be her home for the remainder of her remarkable life except for the last five years spent in Baltimore.

From earliest childhood, Maggie was tutored by her own brilliant father. She was obviously born to be a writer. Words, eloquently spoken or written, fascinated her. Maggie played at manipulating human language and never tired of writing down her thoughts. Then she would rephrase and rewrite the thought until the sequence and the meter seemed agreeable. Thus our small heroine gradually developed into the "poetess of the South." From the highland village of Rockbridge County her poetic creations eventually spread across the world.

Maggie's younger sister Eleanor married an eccentric VMI professor named Thomas Jackson, later known as "Stonewall Jackson." Fourteen months after the marriage Ellie died during delivery of a stillborn child. Shared agony drew together the broken-hearted professor and his grieving sister-in-law. Their once-cool relationship deepened into love. Thomas and Margaret probably would have married, had they not both been devout Presbyterians. The church's *Confession of Faith* explicitly condemned any man who would marry his deceased wife's sister. The rule was finally abandoned near the beginning of the twentieth century, too late for the frustrated couple.

The course of life changed abruptly for Maggie when her close friend Sally Preston died. Sally was the wife of John Preston, another flamboyant VMI professor. Sally and John had seven children. The young mother had a premonition that her final pregnancy would end in death. She urged that if it happened, Margaret Junkin was to take her place. Sally's prediction came true. Major Preston was blinded by grief for many months but finally began to see some promise of renewed happiness in the lovely Margaret. He courted her fervently. Finally Maggie consented, despite her oft-expressed vow never to marry a widowed man, especially if he had children. She was thirty-eight years old, and he was forty-seven.

The marriage proved to be a great source of happiness for Maggie, John, and his children. One year later, in July of 1858, Maggie gave birth to her first child whom she named George Junkin. Two years later she delivered another healthy son, her second and last child. The diminutive poetess, who had earlier resigned herself to life as a spinster, was now in charge of a most prominent Lexington household. With a family of eleven to care for there was little time for writing.

The Civil War forced Maggie to take up her art again. Margaret Junkin Preston produced and published her most widely acclaimed book, *Beechenbrook, A Rhyme of War*. (What is Beechenbrook? Today we call the area "Jordan's Point," at Lexington under the cliffs of Maury River, formerly called North River.) The book proved to be popular, and went through eight printings. With the profits, Margaret built Beechenbrook Presbyterian Church. The quaint gothic structure still stands in 2007 but is no longer a church. It can be seen on the rocky slope overlooking Jordan's Point Park near the south end of the East Lexington Bridge. There is no marker to identify it or to preserve its history of ministry to the busy dockworkers when Lexington was a port on the North River Canal.

Maggie loved Lexington. Her graceful writings sing of the beauty of Rockbridge. She describes the people as extraordinarily loving. The social whirl of Paris had less attraction for her than the nature trails along her neighborhood river. When tragedies came, as happened far too often, Maggie would seek the seclusion of the forest and there find therapy in writing. Our small heroine had cared for her dying mother, then her sister Ellie. Her distinguished father had been forced to leave Lexington forever because of his resistance to Virginia's secession in 1861. Her sister Julia's boyfriend was murdered at the door of the Lexington Presbyterian Church one Sunday morning while Julia sat in the pew waiting. Her brother-in-law, Stonewall Jackson, died in the war. Four of Colonel Preston's children, strongly attached to their stepmother Maggie, died in the first years of her marriage. Maggie's poems poured forth constantly, a moving mixture of pathos and power.

I urge you to read *Beechenbrook* and weep. Read also Margaret's biography written by Mary Coulling, another gifted Lexington author. Drive to Jordan's Point and look at the Beechenbrook

Church. We should not permit the eloquence of Maggie Preston to disappear after she has done so much for us.

When you visit historic Oxford Church, be aware that Maggie's husband John Preston, an avid sportsman, loved our streams and forests. He hunted and fished regularly with Bob Hamilton, founder of Hamilton School just upstream from this church. The Oxford name would have sounded familiar to Maggie. Before moving to Rockbridge, she had lived in both Oxford, Ohio, and Oxford, Pennsylvania. Maggie wrote eighteen hymns for the *Voice Of Praise*, a songbook used at Oxford Church and most other Presbyterian churches a century ago. She also produced church school literature for children. We are indebted to this noble Christian lady, Margaret Junkin Preston.

Lesson 27:
Cyrus Hall McCormick and His World Revolution

For several thousand years, the technique for harvesting grain remained unchanged in the world. On the slopes around Bethlehem, Jesus watched as laborers grasped handfuls of stalks and sliced them off by hand using sickles. In the year 1800 here at Oxford, our farmers did it exactly the same way. Long handled grain cradles were slowly replacing the shorter sickle, but the task remained very labor intensive. This was hard work. However, a Presbyterian boy from Rockbridge County, Virginia would change all that in one generation.

Cyrus Hall McCormick

Cyrus Hall McCormick was born February 15, 1809, on a farm at Steeles Tavern, Virginia. Life was still primitive in those days, but Cyrus was blessed with several advantages. He grew up beside the Great Valley Road. He was taught his history and his heritage. He learned of Benjamin Borden's first meeting with John McDowell near the McCormick home on the upper branches of the James River, near present-day Raphine. He had industrious parents, serious Presbyterians gifted with innovation. His father Robert had married Mary Ann Hall. Her name gives us our connection with Oxford Church, which grew out of Hall's Meeting House. Robert and Mary Ann did not care for Rev. William Graham's new hymn singing, so they gave land, labor, and money to construct Old Providence Church, where to this day Old Testament psalms are sung.

Young Cyrus worked the land, helping to plant and harvest crops in the old, slow, sweaty way. His inventive brain persistently urged him that "there must be a better way." At age 15, he created his own version of the grain cradle that was easier to use than larger models. But the work was still far too slow and difficult. Cyrus' own father Robert had envisioned a horse-drawn machine for cutting standing grain, but he had not succeeded in building a working model. Cyrus resolved to make his father's dream come true.

The task was not an easy one. His many failures brought stinging disappointment. Neighbors caustically suggested that Cyrus should stop his tinkering, get into the field, and accomplish something worthwhile. Common sense told them that the rotary power of a horse-drawn wheel simply could not be converted into rapid reciprocating force. But Cyrus persisted, and with the aid of a gifted blacksmith and the steady guidance of his father, he finally achieved success. He designed a cutter bar with flashing back-and-forth teeth and attached it to a large traction wheel. A steady horse could pull the device and cut standing crops one swath at a time all day long.

Cyrus Hall McCormick statue on the campus of Washington and Lee University.

Thus the agricultural revolution began, in Rockbridge. From 1839 to 1847, Cyrus McCormick manufactured his machine at the Steeles Tavern home farm. Sales were slow in the beginning, and Cyrus realized he must expand his market. He became a salesman. He took his "Virginia Reaper" on a tour of the Midwest where land was level, limestone rocks did not jut out in the field, and labor was scarce. He quickly recognized the grand possibilities that the Great Plains had to offer. Contrary to the advice of his Rockbridge family, Cyrus moved to a village named Chicago. The industry he started there is one of the reasons that little muddy town on the lake grew into the agricultural hub of planet Earth. At last, thousands of acres could be harvested!

McCormick managed, through constant innovation, to stay ahead of the competition. His early machines were considered miraculous, with their ability to mow down standing crops. He next developed a better, larger device that could not only cut but also bind sheaves. Finally, he devised a monster machine that would cut, thresh, winnow, and bag grain in one smooth sweep across a mile-long field. This machine, pulled by multiple teams of horses, removed all limits to the size of grain fields. Food supplies in America could at last keep pace with all population growth.

The "Virginia Reaper" made its way to every country on earth, forever changing the once laborious process of harvesting crops. Wealth, honor, and acclaim were heaped upon Cyrus McCormick while he lived. Nations across Europe awarded him their highest honors, recognizing him as having done more for the cause of food production than any other man. American historians agree. One famous quote: "No general or consul drawn in a chariot through the streets of Rome by order of the Senate ever conferred upon mankind benefits so great as he who thus vindicated the genius of our country." I wish he had said "the genius of Rockbridge County."

During Cyrus McCormick's lifetime, his astonishing inventions touched every part of the world. His cutting bar has been used without significant change for the past one-hundred-and-fifty years. On a smaller scale, barbers and sheep shearers use the same mechanical concept. Mowing hair is quite similar to mowing grain.

Cyrus McCormick, our neighbor boy, never forgot his Rockbridge roots. He gave generously to Washington and Lee University, where a bronze statue perpetuates his memory. When you visit the McCormick homeplace and museum at the Raphine interchange of I-81-64, be aware that just over the hill is another memorial not listed in the brochures—the quaint, stone Old Providence Church. This lovely old meeting house and its graveyard have both been restored. Cyrus McCormick's forebears lie there. Just across the street is Old Providence Associate Reformed Presbyterian Church, the new brick church that was designed and built with McCormick money. Go and visit history...the old stone building is kept open, immaculate, and air-conditioned year round, secluded amongst the fertile hills. Go... look and appreciate...and remember. It is part of your heritage.

Think about this: wherever you may be in the world, the bread you enjoy has in all probability come to the table in some measure through the untiring effort of Cyrus Hall McCormick. He changed the world. Now it is your turn.

Lesson 28:
The Skinner War

In 1841, by all normal measurements, the Lexington Presbyterian Church appeared to be moving into a golden period. The people were proud of their handsome young pastor John Skinner, whom they had called from Scotland. He carried sparkling credentials: degrees from both Edinburgh and Glasgow universities, plus glowing letters of praise from Scottish churches he had served. Everyone seemed charmed by his dignity, his self-assurance, his good looks, and his Old World manner of speech.

The relationship went well for five years. Rev. Skinner served on a number of important Presbytery committees. One of those committees had to decide upon a thorny issue: Which church on Buffalo should survive...Oxford or Collierstown? The Scotsman helped mediate a working solution whereby both churches would continue. But in his own flock, trouble was brewing. In August of 1847, eight prominent members of the Lexington church delivered a letter to the Session, or governing body. They announced "growing dissatisfaction with Dr. Skinner on the part of the congregation." He preached too long, they complained, with subject matter that was cold, tedious, and uninteresting. His voice grated unpleasantly, despite the Scottish accent. Furthermore, he persistently harassed the congregation with demands for more money to be donated to his favorite charities. From the pulpit he would ridicule small gifts, publicly announcing names and amounts. Perhaps such behavior had been tolerated in Scotland, but it was absolutely unacceptable in Rockbridge, the historic seat of religious freedom.

The letter enraged Dr. Skinner. It struck him as worse than disrespectful; it was insulting. He threw caution to the wind. Believing that Presbytery would give him unqualified support, he threatened to resign unless the complaint was immediately retracted. He was mistaken. Instead of censuring Skinner's "enemies," Presbytery wisely began investigating the minister, and a curiosity came to light: the eloquent pastor had published a pamphlet charging many of the church people with offensive and anti-Christian behavior. He was strangely unaware of the fury and embarrassment that could and did result. No one had cautioned him that in Lexington, Virginia, of all places, a recently arrived outsider should think long and carefully before assaulting the integrity of the town's most honored leaders. They reacted by publishing their own response in the *Lexington Gazette*, as well as in Washington and New York newspapers. Among other charges, they called the reverend a liar.

The Skinner War had begun. People took sides. Tempers flared. The entire community buzzed like a jolted beehive. Methodists and Baptists were quickly drawn into the conflict, and finally the Episcopalians. The angry man of God would not soften. From his pulpit came stormy sermons every Sunday. Instead of producing repentance, his words incited wrath and rebellion among the hearers. Supposing the young ladies were the source of criticism regarding the length of his sermons, Dr. Skinner blazed forth with these inspired words: "Nothing is more odious than to witness a young woman enter the house of God, bundled in robes and ribbons, and strange stuffings pinned and padded about her person, so that she must have spent two hours dressing rather than on her knees preparing herself to find the service of her minister to be sweet rather than tedious."

The angry parson found everybody to be at fault except himself. His rage fell publicly on persons of high and low rank. He denounced other pastors in the town, as well as professors at Washington College and Virginia Military Institute. He went so far as to blast the highly revered superintendent of the military school, Col. Francis Smith, because the annual VMI ball was allowed. Skinner did not approve of such entertainment.

The man of God desperately sought allies in his battle with the Lexington church. He turned to the civil court system and attempted to secure a grand jury indictment against his own ruling elders who governed the local church. The court refused. Skinner then took his case to the floor of Presbytery, where he hotly condemned his own congregation as well as the general population of Lexington. The church trial occupies an unprecedented space in the official minutes of Presbytery: 332 pages.

The faithful women of the church in the Lexington parish had been Skinner's most loyal supporters. At first, they found him stimulating and attractive. No sacrifice was too great in honor of their spiritual leader. He wanted a new manse to live in. He wanted a new church built downtown. He got both, thanks to the sewing and cooking and sacrificing of the devout women. They bought and paid for the land. Did their lofty parson bend his knee in gratitude? Not exactly. Reverend Skinner wrote, "I am slandered for permitting my church to be under 'Petticoat Government'." Surely such a statement drove the final nail in the coffin. Skinner had crossed the line.

After months of hearings, Presbytery voted overwhelmingly to sever Skinner's connection with the Lexington Presbyterian Church and, further, to strip him of his license to preach anywhere. The action was drastic and extraordinary. Dr. Skinner appealed his case to the higher church courts. At the end, he was finally allowed to continue as a Presbyterian preacher. He stormed out of lovely Rockbridge, never to return. Records indicate that he enjoyed some success as a pastor in Canada.

What had gone wrong in Lexington? It seems obvious that there was a clash of culture between the parson and his community. On all sides, anger generated into rage, which degenerated into mental incompetence. Well-intentioned followers in such cases abandon the Prince of Peace and resort to fierce hostility, to the detriment of the church. This lesson ends, however, with good news. Lexington Presbyterian Church survived. A benevolent God sent them the Reverend William S. White, who for many years was the most loving and wise good shepherd any congregation could desire.

Lesson 29:
General Lee Comes to Rockbridge

Gen. Robert Edward Lee is the most celebrated hero of southern America. Does it not seem strange that he would choose to finish out his life in a mountain village that he had never before seen? This remarkable leader could have chosen any address in the southland as his postwar home, and he would have been welcomed with enthusiasm.

After the Appomattox surrender, the Lee family situation was heartbreaking. The victorious federal government had confiscated all 1,300 acres of their real estate, including their beautiful Arlington mansion. General Lee was getting

Robert E. Lee at Washington College

old and was not in good health. Not only was he now unemployed, he was under indictment and subject to imprisonment. Some radicals wanted him to be hanged. In a borrowed tenant house outside Richmond, the Lees considered their frightening future.

To that tenant house rode Judge Brockenbrough from Lexington, Virginia, dressed in a borrowed suit of clothes. He introduced himself to General Lee, and offered the old soldier a job. "Come and be president of Washington College," he encouraged Lee. "We have no money and almost no students, but you can make a difference." In what now seems to be a miraculous answer, General Lee said yes. The acceptance was not immediate. He asked some painful questions: "My age and my health are working against me. I have life-threatening legal problems. How

can I teach young men to respect civil authority when I may be imprisoned at any time? I may not be an asset to your college." The trustees of Lexington's little college were willing to gamble. The contract was signed. The handsome white-haired warrior saddled his beloved war horse Traveller and rode to Rockbridge.

It is clear that the noble hero wanted work. Honor demanded that he earn a living for his family. Lee prayed that the position at Washington College would allow him to improve young lives and thus make the world a better place. His earnest prayer was answered and fulfilled, continuing to this very day. The college survived. Judge Brockenbrough proved to be a close friend for Lee. He opened a new school of law at the college. He walked from Thorn Hill every day, across town and to the campus, greeting President Lee morning and afternoon.

Surprising coincidences of history helped make Lexington look attractive to Robert E. Lee. He saw the place for the first time in August 1865 as he took on his new job, but fate was drawing some threads together. His son Custis, only weeks earlier, had eagerly accepted an offer from VMI to be a professor there. Father and son would be together. More intriguing is the odd action of Virginia's General Assembly early in 1861. It ordered that the body of Henry Lee be brought from Georgia and re-interred in Virginia, in of all places, Lexington! Henry, nicknamed "Light-horse Harry Lee" and hero of the American Revolution, was Robert E. Lee's father. The Civil War violently interrupted transfer of Henry's body, but Lee knew it would one day be accomplished. Lexington, Virginia would be home to at least three generations of Lees. It was a breathtaking unfolding of history, unforeseen and unexpected. General Lee also knew that the college in Lexington had been called Liberty Hall. It was named Washington College only after George Washington gave an enormous gift to the school. Lee's own wife was part of the Washington family. Such ties with Lexington must have helped point him toward Rockbridge.

The connections do not end there. Before the Civil War began, General Lee wrote to his wife Mary instructing her to remove from Arlington House the silver, the George Washington letters, and other priceless articles because, he said, "War is inevitable." Guess where those precious trunks were buried: right here in Rockbridge! The Lees had pondered the problem of security and concluded that Lexington, Virginia, was the safest spot. As Mrs. Lee wrote, "It is the most inaccessible place I know of." With the hindsight of history I can say, "Be nice, Mrs. Lee. That inaccessible place is where you will be lying forever." The poor lady had no inkling that she and her family would end up here.

She was not quite correct about Lexington's inaccessibility either. General Hunter and 1,800 troops found it easily enough one June morning in 1862, taking everything along the way. But the trunks from Arlington were not discovered. General Lee knew that upon his arrival, the family valuables would be dug up. Mary had written a note to Francis Smith at VMI. "I thank you for your care of our silver and papers. Can they be safe where they are until the close of the war? I would like to preserve the only relics left of our once happy home." Those trunks contained articles and papers and silver not only from Arlington House but also from Mt. Vernon, home of George Washington. The Father of our Country had an adopted son who was his wife Martha's grandson by her first marriage. He was George Washington Parke Custis, Mary Lee's father. It staggers the mind to realize that the worldly goods of the aristocratic Lee and Washington families were successfully preserved under a barn floor near Fairfield, Virginia, a few miles outside Lexington.

History had also conspired to bring Thomas Jonathon Jackson to Lexington prior to the war. Lee knew that his powerful compatriot's body now lay in the little town. These are some of the surprising elements that combined to bring Robert E. Lee to Rockbridge. Lee interpreted the opening doors as acts of divine providence guiding him to this place.

What is Lee's connection with Oxford Church? There are several. Oxford's pastor, William Graham, founded Washington College. Without Graham, there would have been no job offered to Lee. Without Robert E. Lee, the college would probably not have survived. Without the college, Oxford Church may not have survived either. Through more than two centuries the college has provided life-saving leadership to Oxford. That school has educated some of her pastors, including the late Dr. Diehl. Without the Lexington college, now Washington and Lee University, I myself would not be in Oxford's pulpit as your present pastor, nor would I be writing these history lessons for you. Intriguing connections, most would be forced to agree.

Lesson 30:
Lee in Lexington: Why Did They Love Him So?

When Gen. Robert E. Lee decided to live in Lexington, many influential friends were shocked and dismayed. They honestly felt that by moving to such an unknown spot, Lee's impact on history would evaporate. They were wrong, thank God. From his modest office at Washington College, the vanquished warrior did more to calm seething hostility, North and South, than any other American. How? Not by making speeches, not by using the major media of his day. Lee succeeded by simple, quiet example.

As soon as the agonizing surrender was behind him, Lee set a course from which he never deviated. He wrote, "It is now the duty of every citizen to do all in his power to aid in the restoration of harmony and peace and in no way oppose the policy of the General Government." Those clear and unequivocal words came not from some ivory tower. They came from a noble man who had been heavily victimized by that "General Government." Every inch of his real property had been stripped away. He was never allowed to vote or to hold public office, but the emancipated slaves were allowed both. Normal people reacted with bitter resentment and murderous hatred. To every one of them General Lee said, "Put it behind you. Sign the oath of allegiance. Move forward toward rebuilding our broken land. It is your duty." (Notice how often that word "duty" appears.) Sincere people nearly choked on such a demand. Yet if Lee could do it, some of the others could, too. It took time.

Do not hold the impression that Robert E. Lee was a pushover. Northern soldiers knew quite well what he could accomplish despite insurmountable obstacles. Lee never lost that steel determination. His was a subtle power, emanating from within. Arriving at Washington College in September 1865, Lee instantly plunged into the new job as president. There were only forty students. There was no cash, except what the desperate trustees could borrow. When word spread that General Lee was in command of the school, another one hundred students signed on.

Most of them were battle-scarred veterans. Who on earth could even manage such a wild and reckless pack, much less teach them liberal arts? Could this sick and aging gray-haired aristocrat from the rolling Piedmont find a way? Remarkably, he did. Lee's technique varied from man to man. Some of the bearded, troublesome veterans would leave President Lee's office with tears streaming after he softly reminded them that their mothers back home were cherishing great expectations and praying daily for their sons. Continued the General, "And I also pray for you."

He used a different stroke when a student who had been called in appeared chewing tobacco. Lee politely asked him to dispose of the quid. The young man stepped outside, spat, and returned with the bulge still in his cheek. Motioning him to sit, Lee silently wrote a note, handed it over and said, "Read this, and take it to the registrar." The curious student read what he held in his hand. There was his full name, followed by "will be leaving our campus today, because of disrespect for the college president." Everybody quickly learned that discipline from Lee was just and it was final. There were no appeals.

The college came alive. Money began to flow in, beginning with $15,000 from Cyrus McCormick who was now living in Chicago. Great wealth had not caused McCormick to forget his roots in Rockbridge. Other gifts totaling more than $100,000 were received in the first ten months of Lee's presidency. Most of the cash came from the industrial North. Enmity was forgotten, giving way to admiration. By the second school year four hundred students had enrolled, making their way to Lexington from the North as well as the South. They do so yet.

Construction began on Lee Chapel, an absolute priority for the new college president. He wanted his office placed in the chapel, and it soon came to be. Lee was surprised at how much he loved his new job. He had come here thinking it would be temporary and that he would soon move to a farm somewhere east, away from the mountains. He had changed the school, but the school had changed him too. He later wrote, "The big mistake of my life was choosing a military career." This surprises us. Even in defeat, General Lee stands in history as a heroic military figure. In his later years, he believed he should have devoted his life to education.

The Kappa Alpha fraternity began in Lexington, formed by a few earnest students who saw in General Lee the finest hope for mankind. It is the only fraternity in the world dedicated to emulating one man, Robert E. Lee. From Lexington, Virginia, that fraternity has spread to 115 colleges and universities and claims 70,000 living members.

Why do people love Lee so? The answer can be summed up in one word: character. The world loves someone who can be trusted. General Lee was propelled by one motive—his unremitting sense of duty to do the right thing. People could disagree with his idea of what was the "right thing." They could not quarrel with his motivation.

Every Christian church shares Lee's noble goal. This adds one more connection between Oxford Church and Robert E. Lee. Whenever I hear disparaging remarks made about the noble man, I think of the words of Jesus: "Father forgive them. They know not what they do."

Lesson 31:
The Religion of Robert E. Lee

General Lee spent the final years of his life at Lexington, Virginia, a stronghold of Presbyterianism. He rests there to this day. However, his beginnings lay east of our mountains, in the country of wealthy Tidewater plantations. Most of those planters were members of the established Church of England, or Anglican persuasion. After the American Revolution, they remained in that denomination now called Episcopal Church of America, in contrast to the Scot-Irish dissenters, most of whom were Presbyterian.

Throughout his life Lee was an active member of the Episcopal Church, giving generously of his time, money, and leadership. On his last healthy day Lee chaired a meeting of the vestry at his Lexington church. The church treasurer reported a deficit in regard to the pastor's salary. Lee's body was failing by that hour in the evening, but in a voice barely audible he said, "I will give that additional sum." It may have been the last complete sentence he ever uttered. Walking the few steps to his home, he collapsed, never to rise again. Death came a few days later.

General Lee's son wrote some years afterward, "Father had a practical, everyday religion which supported him all through his life. It enabled him to bear with equanimity every reverse of fortune, and to accept good fortune without undue elation." I have found in Lee's personal letters some proof of the accuracy of that assessment. One example is seen in his letter to his wife Mary after the Union forces had confiscated the beautiful Lee home, Arlington House: "I fear, dearest Mary, we have not been grateful enough for the happiness there within reach, and our Heavenly Father has found it necessary to deprive us of what He had given. I acknowledge my ingratitude and my unworthiness, and submit with resignation to what He thinks proper to inflict upon me. We must trust all to Him." Instead of blaming God for misfortune, Lee is clearly saying "Thy will be done. We deserve whatever God lays upon us."

When his son Fitzhugh was wounded and then captured, General Lee wrote to his wife: "I have heard with great grief that Fitzhugh has been captured by the enemy. We must bear this additional affliction with fortitude and resignation, and not repine at the will of God. It will eventuate in some good that we know not of now."

Troubles multiplied as the relentless fury of war swirled around the great man. Fitzhugh's wife Charlotte died while her husband lay in a Union prison. Here is how General Lee dealt with that blow. Writing once again to Mary, he sent these words of comfort:

> It has pleased God to take from us one exceedingly dear to us, and we must accept His holy will. Charlotte will, I trust, enjoy peace and happiness forever. What a glorious thought, that she has joined her little cherubs and our angel Annie [Lee's deceased daughter] in heaven. Link by link the strong chains that bind us to earth are broken and our passage smoothed to another world. Oh that we may be at last united in that heaven of rest, to join in an everlasting chorus of praise and glory to our Lord and Saviour. I grieve for the anguish her death brings to our dear son, and the pain it brings to the bars of his prison. May God in His mercy enable Fitzhugh to bear the blow so suddenly dealt.

While living in Lexington after the war, Lee determined to visit the grave of daughter Annie during the autumn of 1870. She had died while vacationing in North Carolina, and there she was buried. He wrote to Fitzhugh: "I wish to witness her quiet sleep with her dear hands crossed over her breast as in mute prayer, undisturbed by the distance from us, while her pure spirit waits in bliss in the land of the blessed."

In the midst of war in 1863, Jefferson Davis called for a day of prayer and fasting throughout the Confederacy. Lee responded with this order to his troops:

> Soldiers! We have sinned against Almighty God. We have forgotten His signal mercies and have cultivated a revengeful, haughty and boastful spirit. We have not remembered that the defenders of a just cause should be pure in His eyes, and that our times are in His hands. We have relied too much on our own arms for the achievement of our independence. God is our only refuge and strength. Let us humble ourselves before Him. Let us confess our many sins, and beseech Him to give us a higher courage, a purer patriotism and more determined will; that He will convert the hearts of our enemies; that He will hasten the time when war with its sorrows and sufferings shall cease; and that He will give us a time and place among the nations of the world.

I wish there were some way to know what was in the hearts of battle-hardened infantrymen when they heard those astonishing words from their commanding general.

We have to be impressed with Lee's ability to handle catastrophic misfortune. The loss of his real estate, the death of his child, the capture of his son, the agony of defeat...all these things were absorbed without bitterness. When another daughter Agnes hovered near death after the move to Lexington, Lee never faltered. He sat by her side night and day for one month, holding her hand and quietly soothing her fever until she recovered.

If there is a finer earthly model for Christian living than Robert E. Lee, please show me. This dignified and self-contained man would never have been attracted to the flashiness of contemporary television evangelists so popular in our day. He would have been repelled by the demonstrations and the so-called "jerks" that seized some of the faithful during emotional religious revivals. No doubt some of them would have characterized Lee's religion as too sober and stiff. However, it worked for him through good times and bad, up to and including the last hour of his life. He enjoyed great hymns. He committed many of them to memory. He was able to quote from them as well as recite lengthy portions of the Bible in times of great danger.

Our lovely valley has been made richer by the continuing influence of this incomparable Christian gentleman. So has the college he revived...and especially through that college, so has Oxford Presbyterian Church. Thank you, God, for sending such a man to Rockbridge County!

Lesson 32:

Robert E. Lee:
What Should He Have Done?

Those who hold General Lee in high regard are sorely disturbed by the movement to remove his name from Washington and Lee University. In the Summer 2007 issue of the W&L University's alumni magazine there is a letter containing these words: "How far can W&L aspire to rise intellectually and morally when it is named after a man who failed utterly at the most fateful moral issue of his time? Lee was a traitor. But for the grace of General Grant and others he would have stood trial for treason, and been either imprisoned or hung. This is not the type of person a school that aspires to greatness should be named for." The letter is signed by a graduate of W&L, class of 1965.

My question to the writer: What would you have done, had you been faced with Lee's dilemma in 1861? Robert E. Lee was a professional soldier. He strongly opposed Virginia's secession. But the state's leaders took action to secede and be independent of federal authority. Lee was suddenly forced to make a terrible decision. He knew that war was inevitable. He had only two choices: either attack the state where his roots ran deep, or defend its position. After an inner debate that tortured his very soul, Lee declared, "I cannot under any circumstance, lift my sword against my homeland, my native Virginia and my family." Such a wrenching decision should never be labeled "utter moral failure." Lee followed the voice of his conscience. He did what he perceived as his duty.

When George Washington elected to wage war against the British Crown whom he had sworn to defend, was that moral failure? The king certainly thought so. If America had been defeated, Washington probably would have been hung. Using the above letter writer's logic, should a school be named after this type of person? If we must remove the name of Lee, then why not also remove Washington? And where do we end the cleansing? Our nation's capitol must be renamed, as well as a state and countless other namesake cities and institutions.

Although Lee's family had owned slaves, as had Washington's, Robert E. Lee had freed all those whom he had the power to free, years before the Emancipation Proclamation. Does that not count toward his moral redemption? In none of his writings do we find Lee supporting the cause of slavery. There are some people today who choose to think the American Civil War began and ended over the single issue of slavery. My own ancestors living in northern Pennsylvania fought on the side of the Union. And I ask a reasonable question: Would several hundred thousand southern men volunteer to give their lives in defense of slavery when only three percent of the population owned slaves? Of course not. Although we can never dismiss the evils of slavery, other vital issues were involved.

The serious student of history learns that all great moments and great movements are complex. One must not judge too hastily the motivation of others, whether the subject is war or religion or even the choice of a mate. Historians tell us that our war against England in the 1770s was never supported by more than one third of the American population. Now we call it our Revolutionary War, through which we won our nation's independence. Hindsight portrays it as a noble cause, yet while the war was being waged, the majority of our people opposed it.

Robert E. Lee spoke of the Civil War in America as a tragedy. Few people today would disagree with his assessment. Surely some alternative could have been worked out. But the war happened. Sincere citizens on both sides gave all they had in support of their convictions. When that terrible war finally ended, one great man did more than any other to restore harmony and peace and loyalty to the government. His name: Robert E. Lee, the defeated southern commander.

What has this lesson to do with Oxford Church? The answer is easy. The roots of Washington and Lee University and Oxford

Church are identical. The same Presbyterian leaders established both institutions. Their histories are intertwined for a quarter of a millennium. To be interested in one is to be interested in both. Robert E. Lee helped insure the survival of the school that has always provided leadership for Oxford Church. Therefore, we do well to keep the banner of his name held aloft. There is no finer example of Christian nobility.

Lesson 33:
Let's Not Forget Traveller

What is the connection between Oxford Church and the aging war-horse named Traveller? Here are some answers. That great stallion survived a war and carried his famous master, Robert E. Lee, to Rockbridge County. General Lee resuscitated Washington College, and that institution helped ensure the survival of this church.

In Lexington, Lee took time to write a description of Traveller in response to the request of a distant artist:

> If I were an artist like you I would draw a picture of Traveller, representing his fine proportions, muscular figure, deep chest and short back, strong haunches, flat legs, small head, broad forehead, delicate ears, quick eyes, small feet, and black mane and tail. Such a picture would inspire a poet, whose genius could then depict his worth and describe his endurance of toil, hunger, thirst, heat, cold, danger, and suffering. He could enlarge upon his sagacity and affection, and his invariable response to every wish of his rider. He might even imagine his thoughts, through the long night marches and days of battle through which he has passed. I purchased him in the mountains of Virginia in the autumn of 1861, and he has been my patient follower ever since— to Georgia, the Carolinas, and back to Virginia. He carried me through the Seven Days battle around Richmond, the second Manassas, at Sharpsburg, to Fredericksburg, Chancellorsville, Gettysburg and back to the Rappahannock. From the commencement of the campaign in 1864 at Orange till its close around Petersburg, the saddle was scarcely off his

back as he passed through the fire of the Wilderness, Spotsylvania, Cold Harbour, and across the James River. In the campaign of 1865 he bore me from Petersburg to the final days at Appomattox Court House. You must know the comfort he is to me in my present situation. You can, I am sure from what I have said, paint his portrait.

Genuine affection bonded Lee and his horse. One day at the East Lexington boat landing, Traveller got loose while Lee was visiting aboard a luxury craft. People tried to catch the horse but failed. When they made General Lee aware of the problem, he stepped out on the deck, spotted his rapidly disappearing steed, and gave a low whistle. The horse stopped. The pursuers stood still. Lee repeated the soft whistle. Instantly Traveller answered with a glad whinny, turned and ran back to his beloved master who by then had come ashore.

Lee's son, Robert E. Lee Jr., writes that during a review of troops near Orange Court House in 1863, his father allowed the strong horse to set his own pace for the nine-mile ride around the army. Traveller loved to run. His rapid lope never slackened throughout the review. Of the dozen or more mounted officers trying to accompany General Lee, none made it to the finish line with him. They could only listen to the roar of distant cheering as soldiers hailed their hero.

It obviously took a number of miracles to bring a man so great as Robert E. Lee to Rockbridge and to keep him here. Traveller, the great gray horse, must be included in the list of miracles.

We know that General Lee and Traveller both watched the construction of the building that shelters us today—the brick church of Oxford. Lee was a member of the Episcopal Church, but took great interest in all the local Christian churches. I take pride in the knowledge that as I drive over the crest of Kyger Hill I am traversing the path followed by two extraordinary heroes, Lee and Traveller. I am viewing the same magnificent scenery that they enjoyed, the same mountains and the same streams. I try to absorb the heritage, hoping that some of Lee's spirit and Traveller's can make me strong too.

Go visit the general and his horse where they lie at Lee Chapel, and remember what they did for the college and for Rockbridge. We are indebted to them, and to God for sending them here to us.

Traveller's grave on the west side of Lee Chapel on
Washington and Lee University campus.

Lesson 34:
Stonewall Jackson: He Was Driven

Success and fame, for some heroes, seems to come upon them as a gentle gift from heaven. From early childhood they do things correctly on the first attempt, with no apparent training. Thomas Jonathan Jackson was not so fortunate. Although no man in Rockbridge was more determined to succeed than he, Jackson's eventual success came only after the expenditure of enormous effort.

Born in 1824 and orphaned by age seven, Tom Jackson was shuffled from home to home as he grew up among his relatives. At age eighteen he entered West Point Academy. What sustained him? The childhood memory of his mother's prayers. Her young life had ended abruptly, but her influence endured throughout the entire lifetime of her son. Jackson came to Lexington in 1851 as an instructor at Virginia Military Institute. His outstanding service as a soldier in Mexico plus his phenomenal mental capacity had won recognition among American military leaders.

Rockbridge delighted Jackson. He wrote glowingly of the unsurpassed natural scenery, even before he viewed Oxford Valley from the top of Kyger Hill. Here was a professional soldier who longed to put down roots. He earnestly desired a secure family situation. In Lexington he would finally have the blessing that had been denied him in childhood. He would have a home. Tom Jackson married Eleanor Junkin in 1853 and moved into her home, the large "president's house" on the campus of Washington College. After the distinguished Junkin family adjusted to Jackson's numerous eccentricities, they learned to love him. How was he different? The short answer would have to be: in every way. He marched to his own drummer. For example, Jackson followed a schedule that was fixed in his mind, and nothing would cause him to deviate. In the midst of the most exciting conversation at the Junkin fireside after supper, Jackson would abruptly go to his room at the first stroke of the hour, which his brain told him was his time for study. The Junkins and their guests would be left looking at each other in wonderment. Eleanor's older sister Margaret lived there. She wrote vivid accounts of Jackson's impact on Lexington. Be aware, Margaret later became Mrs. J.T.L. Preston, but not before she had developed an intense relationship with Stonewall after Eleanor's untimely death. Margaret's writing won for her the title "Poet Laureate of the South."

Cadets and students referred to Jackson as "Tom Fool." Only after the major proved to be a Stone Wall in combat did the snickering end. He may have had his peculiarities, but in war he had no match. Throughout his life, Jackson was an absolute health fanatic. He sucked lemons constantly, believing that they added strength and vigor to the body. He refused coffee and tea, not because he found them distasteful but because he found them enjoyable. The same was true for alcohol and tobacco. On hot summer nights it was his practice to soak his sleepshirt in cold water, put it on, and go to bed, to the dismay of his physician who wrote about it. When he walked across the college campuses, he kept one hand in the air above his head to promote blood circulation to his brain. It made him look like something of an idiot perhaps, but it must have worked. No doubt some of his detractors could have benefited from Jackson's unusual notions had they been willing to experiment.

The power of Jackson's intellect was never in doubt. He memorized his class lectures, expounding on difficult mathematical analyses. He flooded the classroom with details about dimensions, motions, and formulae. All of it was clear in his brain. He made the mistake of assuming the students' minds were blessed with similar capabilities. Most were not, and Jackson was not a popular teacher. His immense power of concentration turned him into a most effective warrior, however. As he rode through any countryside his brain recorded every detail of the terrain. He could call up those details in the heat of battle. He ignored enemy bullets and cannonballs because his mind was totally engaged in the next maneuver, and the next. Military skill made Stonewall Jackson a hero. After his death, astonished Lexingtonians watched northern soldiers flock to Jackson's grave to honor their fallen enemy. His tactics have been copied worldwide. Stonewall Jackson found success in life as a soldier.

Most of us have never been told of his other achievements. One notable example is the Sunday school he founded and operated for Lexington slaves. Major Jackson had memorized the Presbyterian catechism. He required those slaves to do the same. It must have been an unpleasant chore for them, but they eagerly came. They quickly learned to arrive on time. Jackson locked the door at the precise time when class began. No latecomers were admitted. At the time it was the slaves' only opportunity for public education. They showed great affection for their stern teacher and called Jackson "the black man's friend." Several of the students achieved high positions. One of them was elected president of Morgan State University in Baltimore. Another served for many years as pastor of the Fifth Avenue Presbyterian Church in Roanoke. His name is familiar to Lexington: Dr. Lylburn Downing.

Jackson began every day with a period of private prayer. Nothing was allowed to interrupt that half hour. Then he took a brisk walk, which was followed by family prayers. Everybody in the household was required to be present, even the guests and the servants. Public prayer was a challenge, however. Reverend White once called on Major Jackson to lead in prayer at the Presbyterian church. The disaster was long remembered by all who were there. The brilliant brain utterly failed. Jackson was able to stammer only a few halting words, then he choked in silence and finally sat down. Embarrassment overcame the whole assembly. The saintly pastor stepped forward and relieved tensions by dismissing the meeting. Word spread throughout the town. Jackson, who demanded perfection from those about him, had performed miserably. The people were delighted with such a morsel of gossip. To this day we recount the event and speak of it and smile. But watch. The great soldier taught himself. By extreme effort of mind and will, Jackson became a forceful public speaker. People would travel for miles to hear his beautiful and moving corporate prayers. Soldiers on the battlefield became Christians through the power of Jackson's clearly enunciated prayers. Black people congregated on his lawn in Lexington so they could overhear his family prayers in the evening.

Few admirers realize that this devout church deacon was also successful in the business world. It is obvious that Jackson was driven to overcome the hardship he endured as an orphan. By careful investment of his modest salary he became a well-to-do citizen of Lexington. He and his second wife Mary Anna Morrison bought the "Jackson House" now recognized as a tourist destination. In addition he bought a small farm on the east edge of town where he produced wheat, corn, and cabbage, and kept a milk cow. He owned as many as nine slaves, six of whom came with his marriage to Mary Anna. Jackson owned one third of the Lexington Tannery, a strong downtown industry. Financial leaders took note. They elected him to the board of the Lexington Savings Institution, as well as the mortgage-lending group called the Lexington Building Fund Association. Jackson was never called "Tom Fool" by the bankers.

He joined the prestigious Franklin Debating Society. Again, after a dismal beginning he worked his way forward from painful, dull speeches to precise and polished presentations. He was elected as one of the twelve original members of the Rockbridge Bible Society. He became a life member of the American Bible Society.

We see in Stonewall Jackson a bashful orphan who by intense persistence realized his ambitions. He had a favorite saying that guided him and can do the same for us. That oft-used Jackson quote is chiseled into the wall of the Virginia Military Institute: "You may do whatever you resolve to do."

Lesson 35:
Those First Rockbridge Churches

The people who chose to settle here in the forks of the James were Presbyterians. They brought their religion with them from Scotland and Ireland. Although physical survival on this dangerous frontier was uppermost on the list of priorities, duty to God seems to have been next. The first worship services took place under large trees or crude arbors. When a settlement showed signs of permanence, log meeting houses were built. On Borden's Grant such buildings first appeared as what we now call Old Providence, Timber Ridge, and New Monmouth churches. During the frightening events of the French and Indian War between 1754 and 1763, those meeting houses were fortified as places of refuge. Oxford's first log building arose then, to serve as meeting house and community fort. Without exception the log structures gave way to stone, some as early as the 1750s. An example is the Timber Ridge stone meeting house that survives today and remains in use with substantial modifications.

Going to church was serious business. Very little provision was made for comfort. The floor was bare earth and the benches were split logs without backrests. Windows were simple openings made by leaving out parts of logs. Stone churches had slightly larger windows, without glass. Before 1800 no heating was allowed. Stern churchmen viewed that comfort as luxury unworthy of a Christian. Physicians also warned that public gatherings in a warm enclosure endangered health.

Preachers delivered two-hour sermons, one before the noon break and one following. The services were not intended as entertainment. Little Samuel Houston endured the Sabbath ordeal by watching wild swallows flutter and compete among the bare rafters of Timber Ridge's stone church. The training must have been worthwhile because he became a famous preacher himself. From Timber Ridge he went to Tennessee to establish the first Presbyterian church in that territory. When he returned to Rockbridge in the 1780s, he gave distinguished leadership to Oxford, Falling Spring, and High Bridge churches. On the east side of Short Hill he lived out his days and wrote of his memories. The pastor and his wife are buried beneath the wall of High Bridge church.

Church interiors did not have the layout we see today. A door provided access at each end of the rectangular room. The pulpit stood high against the center of one long wall. Seating for the congregation was arranged around three sides so that everyone faced the preacher. A large open center aisle allowed space for communion tables which people surrounded only after they had been approved by the session. The sacrament usually lasted two full days.

Preachers were scarce. No one even dreamed that a sermon would be offered every Sunday. People felt fortunate if they could "go to preaching" once a month. On such occasions the pastor would arrive, lean his rifle against the wall, and climb into the pulpit. That signaled the beginning of worship. Rev. Houston wrote of a Sunday at Timber Ridge when a long rifle fell to the floor and discharged. A woman screamed "Indians!" Quite a panic broke out before everyone understood what happened. Order was restored, and the service continued with no harm done.

Church members paid for their seats. We know the practice continued at least into the 1850s, because records show Granville Campbell, one of Old Oxford's leading elders, renting an additional pew for his family in the rival church at Collierstown. Either he was offering financial support for the new church or simply covering all his bases. His strong involvement in both churches continued as long as he lived.

For many years, especially during the existence of Oxford's stone church from 1811 to 1869, congregations in Rockbridge sat in "box pews." Each family would enter the walled enclosure, shut their door, and sit isolated from the view of all except the preacher whose head almost touched the rafters. Church expenses were covered by the rental of pews, so no offertory interrupted the service.

Seats near the pulpit commanded the highest price. Upon entering the church, anyone could discern which members were most prominent and wealthy. Influence was measured by proximity to the preacher. Slaves sat farthest away in back pews that cost nothing. Today one wonders why the front seats are the last to be occupied. What happened? Where are all the wealthy pew-holders? If we were still charging high rents, would some churchgoers give up those back pews and move forward to demonstrate social status?

John Newton Lyle left a written record of his childhood at Timber Ridge church during the 1840s. Box pews reminded him of barn stalls. Once the father closed the pew door there was no getting out. Lyle remembered how children had to be quiet and attentive or "face a lickin' on Monday morning." Respect for the Sabbath day excluded the commotion of bodily punishment, so it was delayed overnight but never forgotten by Timber Ridge fathers.

Some singing could be expected, even required, but there were no hymnbooks and no musical instruments. A man called the precentor or toner, perched only half as high as the preacher, would "give out" one line at a time, to be repeated by the worshippers. The words of the song came straight from the Bible, the book of Psalms. Through years of repetition many of the older members could quote lengthy chapters from the scriptures.

Pastors won distinction in Rockbridge as the primary educational resource. Parents named their babies after the more popular preachers. Virtually all the Presbyterian clergy operated farms and schools. Many became slaveholders, such as Rev. Davidson of Oxford. A few accumulated considerable wealth. Together with the church elders they exercised basic control of society. Respect for these men of God prompted a disproportionate number of Rockbridge boys to enter the ministry.

Choirs, organs, manses, and Christmas pageants did not appear until well into the 1800s, usually evoking a protest and a fight among conservative churchmen. The first limited experiments with Sunday Schools did not begin until after 1830. Weddings took place not in the church but in the home of the bride or wherever the minister could conveniently meet the couple. Rev. Samuel Houston performed a number of marriages on the crest of Short Hill where the old turnpike still cuts through the rocks. The spot was midway between his home and the valleys of Oxford and Buffalo. Houston surpassed all other pastors of his day in the number of couples he united. He may be the source of the popular title, "Marryin' Sam," still used today for pastors who perform marriage ceremonies quite frequently.

The only church function providing a measure of enjoyment was the funeral, which lasted all day and into the night. People brought their finest food, especially cakes. Generous jugs of brandy or whiskey came to be expected, and they were consumed dutifully in honor of the deceased as a sacramental obligation. When Presbytery realized how much fun and frolic had penetrated religion, in classic Calvinist fashion they determined to stamp it out. It took more than a hundred years, but they finally succeeded. Almost. The liquor no longer flows at funerals. However, the wonderful home-baked cakes are another story. Thankfully, they are not yet taboo.

Lesson 36:
The Chapels of Buffalo Valley

Does attendance at church increase your probability of entering heaven? Our ancestors believed the answer was definitely, "Yes." One hundred years ago the Presbyterians of Rockbridge went to church unfailingly. Then they set about making sure everyone else did the same. They built chapels beside every road, no matter how remote. They volunteered prodigious amounts of time and talent as teachers and lay preachers. Oxford Church was typical for the time. There were thirty Presbyterian chapels in the rural parts of Rockbridge County in addition to the sponsoring churches. Other denominations were far less driven. Oxford Church alone was responsible for as many as eight locations, though not all at the same time.

The earliest outpost of Oxford seems to have been "Hamilton's Church," later called Hamilton School. It still stands beside South Buffalo four miles upstream from Oxford. Renowned pastors such as the Reverend Samuel Houston conducted worship services there, as well as weddings and funerals. William Taylor, the famed Methodist Bishop of Africa, preached one of his first sermons at Hamilton's. From 1823 the sturdy log structure served as a community center. Militia held drills on the lawn. Boisterous political rallies were held there. Children attended school at Hamilton's on weekdays. On Sunday they returned for preaching and Bible lessons. Some people called it "Coonskin College." Today the quiet cove displays very little of the liveliness that characterized Hamilton's for nearly two centuries.

Although not founded exclusively by Oxford, its pastors and officers sustained Rapp's Church for more than a hundred years. As late as 2006 Oxford Church furnished a preacher every Sunday. In 2007 Oxford continues to offer Rapp's Church members pastoral care. Although Rapp's is no longer an outpost of any church, the non-denominational place of worship is sustained by residents of the neighborhood as a church school, cemetery, and community center.

The Bolivar Mill School stood very near the Dixon Bridge of Buffalo Creek, within sight of the Murat Post Office. In the late 1800s Oxford began offering preaching and church school there at least two Sundays per month. As late as 1917 Reverend David Lauderdale (for whom the Lauderdale Church in Lexington is named) conducted a revival service at Bolivar, with surprising results. Fifteen people responded by profession of faith and indicated a desire to join a Christian church. Most of them became members of Oxford. The remainder joined Elliott's Hill Methodist and Broad Creek Associate Reformed Presbyterian churches. By 1932 the schoolhouse was closed. The building was moved to Collierstown to become Ralph Hall's country store. I discovered that I have a connection to Bolivar School. The last teacher there was Miss Maybelle Perry, who later joined the staff of Mountain View School and was my delightful fourth grade teacher.

In the 1820s Oxford reached across Meeting House Lane to provide an outpost in Collierstown called Ship Rock Meeting

Rapps Church at 3255 South Buffalo Road.

House. The effort proved so successful as to be alarming. After a decade all Oxford activity centered in Collierstown except for the graveyard. The stone church building was closed. Oxford's communion ware was moved to "New Oxford," and the governing body held session meetings at Ship Rock. After ten years of struggle, the Presbyterians on this side of the hill finally had our church reconstituted as "Old Oxford" in 1843. Ship Rock or "New Oxford" became the Collierstown Presbyterian Church in the 1850s and thrived in the busy commercial activity provided by the Lexington-Covington Turnpike. Travelers between Richmond and Charleston, West Virginia, passed through Collierstown. The church grew and established two additional outposts. One was the Bird Forest Chapel. The other was Unexpected Chapel at the base of Big Hill. I would be remiss if I did not mention Nelson and Gatha Hall, who in 2007 are known as notably active residents of Oxford Valley. Fifty years ago they were primary members of Unexpected Chapel, situated quite close to Gatha's (Reynolds) homeplace.

Another chapel whose existence has come as a recent surprise to me is Woodside Presbyterian Church on Union Run. Established in the 1880s, Woodside had a membership of eighty-two in 1923. The church was dissolved by presbytery in 1957, and the entire congregation was transferred to Oxford Church. Strangely, I can find only one reference to Woodside in Dr. Diehl's history of Oxford. The quaint building stands among trees on property now owned by the Wallin family.

The last Buffalo Chapel on my list has several names: "Oxford Chapel," "Hoge's Chapel," or "The Chapel on Moore's Creek." Situated at the intersection of Blue Grass Trail and Moore's Creek Road, this chapel's interesting story must not be allowed to fade into oblivion. In 1868 the residents of that area (known in 2007 as Oakdale) determined to have their own public school. So they built one, on land donated by the Wilson brothers. The schoolhouse quickly evolved into a popular meeting place for community events. Oxford elders Granville Campbell and

W.F. Johnston established a Sunday school there. Each Sunday afternoon the hills would ring out with the singing from the Bible lessons and the preaching service. The outpost thrived happily until the local Temperance Society adopted it as their meeting place. Their ardent efforts to eliminate the use of adult beverages aroused significant hostility. The new schoolhouse suddenly burned. John Hoge stepped forward, deeding an acre of his land nearby for a replacement structure, stipulating that the building was "to be used as a school, a temperance hall, and a church." Two years later that building also burned to the ground. This time, the message came through: temperance halls were not welcome. So John Hoge deeded another acre to be used for religious services only. A chapel was erected, and it survived.

Major Elhart, L.L. Hotinger, and C.B. Leech kept a Sunday school thriving at Hoge's Chapel for another quarter century. Oxford preachers conducted regular worship several Sunday afternoons a month until the 1930s. In 2007, only a few hardy eyewitnesses are left to tell about the wonderful picnics, the fellowship, and

Woodside Presbyterian Church on Union Run. Church organized in 1887; later disbanded. Property currently owned by Mrs. Margaret Wallin.

the unusually fine singing. The little church was eventually used as a dwelling and finally abandoned, a relic of changing values. Fortunately, there are some things that do not change. The Buffalo area has a legacy of inspired leadership. Dedicated citizens are no doubt waiting in the wings, ready to take on another century of commitment to the most beautiful community in the world.

Does church attendance guarantee you a ticket to heaven? We don't know. But we do know this: recent extensive studies have found that people who go to church regularly live considerably longer than those who do not. For reasons yet unclear, it is a healthy practice and is beneficial to earthly life. The chapels of Buffalo made their contribution long before such facts were revealed.

Lesson 37:
Cruising Down the River

Today we are blessed with such beautiful roads that our minds cannot conceive the conditions faced by the sturdy settlers of Rockbridge County. Until the late 1750s there were very few roads here, so every possession was brought in on a packhorse or carried by individuals. When furniture was required, someone had to make it by hand using an axe. The home itself was the product of this same kind of labor. Yet these Scottish and Irish immigrants survived on harsh frontiers, because they enjoyed liberty.

By the time of the American Revolution, it was clear the settlers were here to stay. They had learned how to provide for themselves and could do so with surplus left over. These surpluses of crops and animals and minerals could be sold, but where? During the early years, Philadelphia was the only answer. It was where these folk had entered America, and for them it remained the major commercial center and gateway to the world. How did they transport hogs and cattle from Oxford to Philadelphia? By foot, through the woods and down the great Indian path that quickly turned into the Great Wagon Road. It sounds impossible but they pulled it off, adding to the list of historical achievements.

Wheels eventually came to Rockbridge, but wheels require roads or at least widened paths. Building roads in the forest is extremely difficult work. Our ancestors apparently did it only when forced to by law. In these 'back parts' they grumbled, "It's my land and I should be allowed to do with it what I wish." Court records bristle with cases where the pioneer was forced to allow travelers passage through his property and with petitions where people wanted roads to their mills and iron works.

Our valley's transportation system took a giant step forward during the mid-1800s in the form of a canal built by the North River Navigation Company. The canal opened Rockbridge to eastern Virginia and the world. Between Lexington and Glasgow, eleven dams were built as well as fourteen boat locks. Society was desperate for easier travel and seemed willing to pay for these improvements at any cost. Even when the price tag reached $30,000 per mile, our ancestors did not relent. Remember, we are speaking of Rockbridge County where the frugal Scot-Irish did not part easily with their money. But they were also farmers, driving livestock to Philadelphia and feeling desperately in need of a more efficient route. The extraordinary project was completed, with the canal in operation by 1861. How I yearn to have witnessed the first boat making its way into the port of Lexington! It is one of the most significant events in this area's history, and it must have been wondrous to behold.

Consider this: a sturdy peddler could carry fifty pounds into Rockbridge on his back; the average packhorse load was two hundred pounds; a good wagon could haul perhaps two thousand pounds when the path was usable. In sharp contrast, suddenly boats were moving smoothly in and out of Lexington, easily transporting 120,000 pounds each! At last, the potential for commerce in our mountain valley was virtually unlimited. Another impossible dream had come true.

Until the canal, it was not easy to get to this area. Our history archives contain countless letters written by people who came here on bone-rattling stagecoaches. The writers all agree: Lexington was hard to reach. Severe discomfort and danger was faced on every trip. While ascending the mountains east and west of Lexington was laborious, descending was heart-stopping. The wooden coach wheels were iron-rimmed, the path was riddled with large rocks, and brakes weren't dependable. Water travel offered something altogether different. It was quiet. It was gentle. Passengers had sleeping quarters on boats one hundred feet long. They were served hot meals and encountered no time-wasting stopovers. A four-dollar ticket on the James River and Kanawha Canal would ease you through the scenic countryside from Lexington to Richmond in less than forty-eight hours. The only sound other than birdsong was the boatman's deep horn alerting the lock-keeper ahead to be up and ready, whether day or night. When traveling on the canal, darkness was not an issue.

When General Robert E. Lee came to Lexington to take charge of the struggling little college here, he rode his horse Traveller. His family came later by boat, and he met them at the wharf early on December 2, 1865. Could his badly crippled wife ever have come to our fair valley without the canal? Probably not. "Beechenbrook" was the name given to the dock area at East Lexington, and General Lee may have smiled at the advertisement that appeared in Lexington's newspaper: "Beechenbrook Flour (from the mill near the dock) will do more to promote family harmony than anything we know of."

What else besides passengers went cruising down the river? The *Lexington Gazette* proudly gives us a list of products from Rockbridge: iron ore, whiskey, brandy, cider, apples, butter, eggs, potatoes, turnips, lime, marble, hemp, leather, wool, beef, pork, mutton, venison, rye, corn, oats, lard, buckwheat, tobacco, hay, vinegar, bark, cement, hoop-poles, fence posts, staves, shingles, plank and scantling, and more. With the canal, farmers could ship their wheat and flour to Richmond—one of the two largest milling cities in the United States. Rockbridge flour was then shipped all over the world.

Local citizens went down to Beechenbrook or Jordan's Point and found they could purchase off the boats virtually anything offered on the world market, right there on the river. Jordan's Point had become a beehive of industrial activity. Factories and foundries, mills and warehouses, shops and stores were all there. These were the shops that would eventually be moved uptown to the Lexington we know today. In November of 1862, William Jordan ran an ad: "Pork Wanted." In finer print he called for farmers to bring him 20,000 pounds of it. That's ten tons! Such huge numbers were undreamed of in pre-canal days.

Railroads came in the 1880s. They proved to be less expensive and more practical than the lovely canal, which slowly closed down and was wiped out by floods. Although in operation for only twenty years, the canal had an unprecedented impact on Rockbridge. All walks of life were affected...from the average citizen to the wealthiest merchant, from the struggling farmer to the hard-working laborer, from the youngest child to the oldest town elder. The canal opened this valley to the east and therefore to the world. Initial construction provided employment for hundreds, and the work was meticulously well done. After more than a century of neglect, beautifully crafted stonework remains intact at the numerous lock sites. We can only dream of the breathless activity that once upon a time changed Rockbridge forever. Think about the covered bridge, the ice plant, the sawmill, and the hat factory. Imagine the music rising from the chartered boat hosting a wedding party. Those were wonderful days for Lexington. It is good to remember and speak of them and to dream of cruising down the river from Beechenbrook toward the ocean.

Lesson 38:
Dr. Zachariah Walker of Brownsburg

For nearly a century New Providence Presbyterian Church was the most prominent rural congregation in Virginia. From its founding in 1756, the Walker family emerged as leaders. The Walkers Creek district is named for them. Alexander Walker was elected elder in that first organizational meeting. His son and grandson kept the heritage intact, serving as strong church officers over the next one hundred years. When squire Joseph Walker's son was born, he was named Zachariah Johnston Walker, after the famous Zachariah Johnston of Rockbridge who helped his friend Thomas Jefferson write documents bringing religious liberty to Virginia and finally to America.

Young Zack was a good student. The New Providence people expected him to make a name for himself in the world. They were not surprised when Zack became a surgeon. They assumed that some day Dr. Zachariah Johnston Walker would become a distinguished elder in the church. Perhaps he would take the seat on the session that his distinguished father had held for forty-six active years.

Dr. Walker's name did begin to appear in the official church records, but not quite as expected. He concluded his service as a surgeon with the 17th Virginia Cavalry during the Civil War and became a physician in Brownsburg, which was then a bustling center of commerce on the main stage route between Lexington and Staunton. Dr. Walker then became involved in the life of New Providence, the church of his ancestors.

The official session minutes strongly suggest that Dr. Walker suffered from a serious personality disorder. Convinced that a neighboring veteran was intent on doing him harm, Dr. Walker attacked the man, Capt. J.J. McBride. The church elders thoroughly investigated the embarrassing incident and found Dr. Walker guilty of conduct unbecoming a Christian. It was the first blot to appear on the noble Walker name. We can imagine how squire Joseph Walker felt. The venerable white-haired father sat on the court that had to reprimand his son. For several Sundays he faced the ordeal of hearing Pastor Junkin read the censure from the pulpit as ordered by the session.

The church elders were good men. They had a duty to encourage repentance and restoration. This time they did not succeed. Their erring church member responded with fury. For the next ten years he fought with his spiritual advisors, demanding a retraction. Brownsburg could not ignore the controversy overshadowing one of their most distinguished families. People took sides, neighbor against neighbor. Dr. Walker fanned the flames, insisting on a church trial at New Providence. In 1879 his eighty-six-year-old father resigned from the session and died heartbroken the same year. At least he was spared the worst, which was yet to come.

Pastor Junkin resigned from the New Providence pulpit and moved to Houston, Texas. The beleaguered elders dropped Dr. Walker's name from the membership roll at his request, but for some reason they ordered black lines drawn around the official record of his lengthy case. This action brought resistance and anger from Dr. Walker. Five years later he was still objecting and fighting to have the case reopened. The new pastor, Clement Read Vaughan inherited a situation that plagued his ministry for most of the ten years he served in Rockbridge.

On Election Day in 1885, Dr. Walker was stabbed by a black man at the polling place in Brownsburg. The doctor survived. His assailant, James Craney, was sentenced to five years in the penitentiary. Upon his release Craney killed a man, resulting in the death penalty, which was carried out in Lexington's jail yard.

More trouble followed Dr. Zachariah Walker. In November of 1889, his neighbor Henry Miller swore out a peace warrant against him. The case would be heard in the courtroom of Brownsburg Academy. To the dismay of Dr. Walker, one of New Providence's elders, Elam Bosworth, presided. During Miller's testimony, Dr. Walker was so enraged that he sprang to the front and stabbed the man to death. Miller's sons reacted instantly with equal violence. One of them drew a handgun and killed Dr. Walker. More shots were fired, and Walker's wife fell dead beside him. Whether she had joined him to attack Miller or to restrain her husband, we do not know. Miller's sons were later tried and acquitted.

The horror of the tragedy apparently did not soften the feelings of the church session toward Zachariah Walker. They refused to allow the couple's funeral at New Providence Church. Their unyielding stand resulted in more conflict, which spread through the congregation and beyond. Newspapers made the most of it, some defending the elders and others condemning them for their disregard of the eminent Walker family history. Even after his death, Dr. Walker remained a serious problem for the church. Pastor Vaughan, no doubt exhausted by the controversy, moved away. Serenity slowly returned to the pastoral community.

More than 30 years before the courtroom tragedy, Oxford's pastor W.W. Trimble resigned the peaceful Buffalo pulpit to help found Brownsburg Academy, back in 1850. Fifteen-year-old Oxford youth W.B.F. Leech enrolled as a boarding student the first year. Little did either of them know that we would be speaking of their school today because the life of a troubled doctor, Zachariah Walker, ended there.

Interesting Note: Today the entire village of Brownsburg is registered as both an historic state landmark and a national historic district, but not because of the Walker story. The unusual distinction was awarded because the appearance has changed so little after more than one hundred years.

Lesson 39:
Rocks, Rills, and Roots at Rapps

As one drives up the South Buffalo Road from Oxford to the Rockbridge County boundary line, the scenery is suggestive of an undisturbed nature trail. Most people would find it hard to believe that this rural byway was once a major north-south traffic artery used first by Indians as a warpath. White settlers moved in during the mid-1700s and gradually widened the trail to accommodate wheeled carts. By 1800 the headwaters of South Buffalo promised to become an industrial complex. Some eight miles upstream from the log fort called Oxford Meeting House, a village appeared. It was centered around a large commercial tannery operated by the high-energy Taylor family, which had won repute for skill in processing animal hide into leather products. Tanbark was needed, tons of it, and families moved in to meet that need, eager for employment in the secluded vale.

A small meeting-house was built across the stream from the tannery. During the day, axes rang out among the hills. Each evening, the plaintive sound of lowing oxen would be heard. Man and beast rested after hard labor of harvesting and transporting forest products from higher elevations. On Sundays hearty singing echoed from the church in the wildwood. At first everybody was Presbyterian. But by 1830 some of the Taylor family had become Methodists...extraordinary Methodists. William Taylor first taught school in the little village beside Buffalo Creek, then moved on to win international distinction as a Methodist preacher and Bishop of Africa. The Taylors called the church "South Buffalo Meeting House" and insisted that it be open to all denominations, especially Presbyterian, the faith of their fathers.

In 1836 Matthias Rapp and his wife Mary Saville bought the property from the Taylors, including the church and cemetery. They built a home across the vale from the tannery and operated a grinding mill that may already have been in place. Matthias wanted a more powerful mill, and he succeeded in designing and building his dream only a short distance from the earlier mill. It was turbine-driven, most unusual for the time, and was capable of driving heavy equipment for sawing and processing timber. The community came to be named Rapp's Mills. Two grocery stores, a post office, two water powered mills (some historians claim three mills), a tannery, two schools, a church, and a cemetery were there, in addition to commercial distilleries and assorted cottage industries.

Matthias and Mary were unusually generous. They took action to deed land right and left for public use, all free. The church, the cemetery, and the schools were all to be owned by the people of the community. Some time in the 1890s, leadership at the Methodist Church's main headquarters determined that the South Buffalo Methodist Meeting House was too dilapidated to repair and must be replaced. Since the deed did not allow any one denomination to claim exclusive title, the Methodist denomination made a reasonable suggestion: "We'll build a new church as close as possible to the old church." The community rose up with a resounding, "No! We will rebuild our own church on the same spot, free of any denominational ties." And they did. The South Buffalo Methodist Church was to be no more. It was an unpleasant time for those who wanted to remain Methodist. They would have to trek over the steep hill to Mt. Horeb Methodist Church, but even there the Methodists were in turmoil. A Yankee pastor was delivering sermons not properly respectful toward the southern cause. The Civil War was still an explosive topic. After all, it had ended only one generation earlier.

By 1903 the Rapp's community had made their dream a reality. The new church stood on the bank beside the road, proud and strong where it belonged. A dedication service was set for the end of October, 1904. A Lexington newspaper, *The Gazette*, covered the story. Services began at 10 a.m. and continued until 7 p.m. The church was packed, with an additional two hundred standing outside. Photographs show the new church interior furnished with pews and pulpit crafted in the Rapp's woodworking shop across the creek. A huge banner above the pulpit proclaimed "Welcome, All Christian Denominations." Pastors participating in the dedication came from Oxford, Mt. Horeb, Collierstown and Fincastle. One noted speaker was Rev. Charles Manly, for whom Manly Memorial Baptist Church in Lexington was later named.

The *Rockbridge County News* of January 20, 1898, has a column describing another intriguing development, "The Onyx Stone Quarry at Rapp's Mills." A tramway, or small railway was under construction to transport stone slabs the short distance to Rapp's Mill, where additional machinery was being set up for cutting and processing stone. "The stone is of many colors. It takes a fine polish and is in demand at good prices for the inside finish of handsome houses and for the tops of tables and other furniture." The same news article refers to the area as "Snakefoot." Another lesson in this book deals with that name.

For more than a century the Rapps Church has served as worship center. During that time the building has been expanded to include kitchen and additional classrooms, making it the community center. For many years Methodists conducted Sunday school each Sabbath morning. Then the Presbyterians would do the same each afternoon. Preaching was provided two Sunday afternoons per month, mostly by pastors from Oxford. On extremely hot days, the resourceful Presbyterians held their assemblies in the coolness of a nearby cave, to the delight of children.

As this lesson is written in the year 2007, Mother Nature is reclaiming Snakefoot. One small grocery store is there yet. Gone are all six of the mills between Rapps and Oxford. Dr. Jim Parsons and his family occupy the ancestral home where Matthias and Mary lived. The church and cemetery remain in fine condition, there among the woods and templed hills, the rocks and rills and roots of Rapps, resting beside the sweet waters of Buffalo.

Lesson 40:
The Mountain Behind Oxford Church

When we exit the front door of Oxford Church, Short Hill is so spectacular, especially in October glory, that we forget about the majestic mountain guarding us to the rear. I speak of Green Hill, towering nearly 2,900 feet above us, standing between Oxford and the Alleghenies. This lesson deals with some events that took place on the north slope of that old mountain.

John and Nancy Green were the pioneers who settled there. Sometime in the early 1800s they built a two-story log home, larger than was customary for the time. With axe and plow and muscle power, they carved out their productive homestead. When their long lives ended in 1892, they were laid to rest in front of the cabin on land they loved. One hundred years later I owned the little graveyard, which was totally overtaken by jungle growth, invisible, and not mentioned in the title search. The discovery came as a complete surprise to me.

In 1956 I had come to Collierstown Presbyterian Church as "supply preacher." It was my last year of seminary. Upon graduation, the church called me as pastor, and it was there I received the rites of ordination and installation. The people were unforgettable in their affection and their patience, doing their best to turn their overly energetic young recruit into a pastor. It was a wonderful time for me. I loved the unsurpassed mountain scenery. Although I moved to a city church in 1961, autumn brought me back to the hills of Buffalo every year with no exception for the next half-century. I became addicted to the lure of wild turkey hunting.

Sometime during the 1980s, my son Dale and I bought a small tract of forest on Black's Creek, where we could camp and hunt. Later on we were able to buy additional acreage that included the sturdy log house. We promptly restored it as our hunting lodge. At that time I was unaware of its history. I only knew that the cabin was pure luxury after sleeping on the ground and camping in snow, wind, and rain. Sitting before a blazing fire, with wintry sleet falling outside, Dale spoke of discovering what he thought was a tombstone in the thicket. My curiosity was aroused. Next morning we crawled through brush on hands and knees, searching. We finally found a number of grave markers with inscriptions. The information spurred my interest in local history that continues to this day. From court records I found that Green Hill was named for John and Nancy Green. Now they were lying forgotten in the jungle. It struck me as sad, but I took no immediate action to improve their situation.

For several years we enjoyed the hikes and hunts on our land, none of which adjoined the nearby Washington-Jefferson National Forest. Across the fence was a large, attractive parcel that had everything: road frontages, streams, open land, timber, views and wildlife. It was bounded by huge national forests. Furthermore, John and Nancy had originally owned all the connecting properties. Subdividing had happened after they both died in 1892. Through a local realtor I learned that a man in Germany currently owned the beautiful piece of land. When contacted, the German stated flatly: "This is my dream of perfect land. I will never consider letting it go." My hope of putting John and Nancy's farm back together seemed to be an impossible dream.

My attention turned to the graveyard near the cabin. Restoring it would be a challenge, but I was determined. I worked at the project for months whenever I had time to make the two hundred mile round trip. As I labored, I sensed that the dozen or so people who lay in the plot were quietly encouraging my use of muscle and machine to clear the heavy canopy and allow daylight into the scene. By late October the project was finished. I wanted my wife Ellen to see the transformation. We drove to Lexington on a Friday evening, checked in at the Sheridan, and made an appointment with my realtor friend for the next day. He was prepared to help us find a residence to buy in town.

The next morning was gorgeous with crisp, beautiful sunshine and breathtaking swaths of autumn color across the landscape. Ellen and I would have time to visit Green Hill before the appointment. We drove through Collierstown and up Green Lane to our property. After a touching visit with John and Nancy, we walked over to the property line, savoring the extraordinary beauty of the German's hillsides. Ellen said, "I really regret that this lovely place cannot be purchased." My rejoinder was that the price would be astronomical even if the owner should decide to sell. We may as well forget it.

However, after we met with the realtor and looked at some houses, I brought up the subject once again, saying to the agent, "If I send that German a sizeable check, isn't there a chance he might agree to allow me 'first refusal' in the event he ever decides to sell?" The realtor said it might be something to try, but probably would not bear fruit for at least another quarter century. I was willing. After lunch I would provide the check.

While Ellen and I were having lunch, my cell phone rang. It was our realtor. He said, "You're not going to believe this. The German has suddenly decided to sell, and our agency is listing that property in one hour." The asking price was one half of what I expected. We immediately signed the contract. Several other buyers signed that same day, but ours was first. We got the property, although subsequent offers far surpassed the original asking price.

We began to wonder how such good fortune had come about. What spirit had brought us to Lexington that particular weekend? What if a different agency had been allowed to list the property? What caused me to inquire at exactly the right moment and even commit to an unpromising option? Truth slowly dawned on us: John and Nancy had assisted our cause, in appreciation for my labor at their gravesites. Skeptical people smile at the notion, even though the New Testament declares with great authority that the ones who have gone before us are watching from the sidelines, cheering us on (Hebrews 11 and 12).

Today in 2007 as you drive up Virginia Rt. 656, which is Green Lane, you are entering John and Nancy's homeplace, consolidated once more. The modest road ends at a scenic hilltop on the mountain behind Oxford Church. From there you can view the powerful north face of Green Hill, the twin peaks of House Mountain, and the sweeping Allegheny range. There you will also see a white sign swinging in the breeze. The sign reads "Greensgift."

Lesson 41:
Bad Day in Rockbridge

The year 1895 was tough for Oxford Church. Granville Campbell, one of her noblest elders, died. Our dear brick church was twenty-five years old. Without Campbell's guidance and commitment, the building would not have stood so proudly upon the hill. Three months before his death, another catastrophe had rocked the community. Rockbridge County's only bank, the Bank of Lexington, had suddenly suffered financial collapse. One wonders if the bank tragedy could have contributed to Campbell's decline and death.

Charles Figgat

On Valentine's Day in 1895, Charles Figgat, highly regarded cashier of the bank, left town on the afternoon train. No one realized at the time that Figgat carried virtually all of the bank's cash with him. A Chicago newspaper bluntly reported, "About the only thing of value he didn't take was the building itself."

Depositers were stunned. Every dollar was hard earned, at a time when currency could be exchanged for gold, dollar for dollar. People who had chosen to entrust their cash to the heavy vault of the institution were left penniless. The county treasury was stripped. Local government came to a halt. Virginia Military Institute was crippled, and professors of Washington and Lee were left empty-handed. From top to bottom of the financial ladder, most of the citizens of Rockbridge were painfully damaged. Oxford Church, along with all other churches in the area, saw contributions plummet. The cash was gone.

Oxford had been contemplating construction of a manse, or pastor's home, the first in the church's history. That dream abruptly stalled. It would have to wait. The pastor, Rev. William Bailey, would continue to live at Bolivar Mills another five years, serving Woodside Presbyterian Church on Union Run as well as Oxford. He continued hoping in vain for his new residence. He had given up and moved on a full two years before the manse was finally built in 1901. The attractive home still sits beside Buffalo Creek in a picturesque pastoral setting across the highway from present-day "Buffalo Trace."

The devastating financial loss was not the only agony. The sturdy country folk were suffering emotional trauma as well. At least one suicide was attributed to the bank disaster. Our Scot-Irish ancestors depended on the sacredness of honesty. Children were sternly taught that your word is your bond. "When you engage in any business, make sure your associates are God-fearing, active churchmen."

Charles Figgat more than measured up. He met all the requirements with impeccable credentials. A Confederate veteran of rank, he had been General Stonewall Jackson's clerk. When the Bank of Lexington opened in 1874, Figgat was enthusiastically chosen as the primary officer, the Cashier. In the ensuing years he had proven himself, even acting as treasurer of the new Robert E. Lee mausoleum. He collected contributions and paid for the famous recumbent statue of Lee at rest. He helped raise money to place the Stonewall Jackson monument in the cemetery. Everybody trusted him. They admired him. On the street they would hand him their cash to be deposited at his convenience.

Figgat was a father-figure and devout churchman. He served as chair of the building committee that erected the new Robert E. Lee Episcopal Church. He was a tireless Christian gentleman, serving as superintendent of the Sunday school for more than twenty years. He was senior warden of the most sophisticated church in town, where General Lee and VMI Superintendent

Francis Smith served with him on the vestry. Respectability cannot reach a higher level.

The Valentine's Day theft shook Rockbridge to her roots. Hundreds of people severed their connections and their commitments to local churches, including Oxford. The mood was ugly. Some of your suffering forefathers silently breathed a prayer: "Thank God, at least, Figgat was not a Presbyterian."

Recriminations ran wild. Some of the hostility turned toward elders of the Lexington Presbyterian Church. Only three years earlier, those men had formed the Lexington Development Company, which had boomed and burst under something of a cloud. Scandalous allegations of fraud from that time now resurfaced, with quite a number of people convinced that Figgat's robbery was another conspiracy to line the elders' pockets even more. Tough but irreverent men of the soil coined a harsh label for the churchmen: "Psalm-singing sons of witches." (The actual word rhymes with "witches.") Fortunately, the charges proved groundless. Figgat had taken the elders' money as well.

The money was never found, although Figgat did resurface four years later, found dead in Colorado. There was no trace of the $180,000. Although he had lived there under the alias of "Charles Miles," his real name was clearly written in his well-worn prayer book beside his body. By some accounts, the death was a suicide.

The *Lexington Gazette* admitted the story reads like fiction, but stark reality made it the "grandest piece of rascality in the history of our state. Lexington won the unenviable reputation before the world as having produced one of the shrewdest bank robbers, a prince of the profession, a Napoleon of Finance."

The good news is that banks all over the country were investigated closely. The wreck in Lexington helped tighten the rules. By the end of 1895, which witnessed the coldest weather in fifty years, our county began to settle back into a fairly normal routine. The people waited for better times. It took a decade, but happy times did come again.

Lesson 42:
Infant Pittsburgh

"Do you know of any other town in America where iron ore is taken from the earth, converted into pig iron at the furnace, and then manufactured into engines, boilers and other machinery, all within the corporate limits?" That question is found on a brochure in 1891, referring not to Pittsburgh or Birmingham or Baltimore, but to a scenic little village that had recently been renamed "Buena Vista." It was in Virginia, nestled against the mountains bordering the Great Valley. The correct answer to the question was, "No." There was no other town that could make such a fantastic claim.

In the year 1889, several local leaders formed themselves into the Buena Vista Company, with the purpose of promoting industry in the level area then known as Hart's Bottom and Green Forest. The fact that the river had created such uncharacteristically smooth land in the hills of Rockbridge did not deter these visionaries. In slightly more than one year they claimed fantastic success. They quintupled the number of houses and businesses, attracting newcomers from far and wide into the flood plain.

The developers soon realized that the name "Hart's Bottom" would have to go. They were inspired by Col. Jordan's iron furnace standing several miles upstream where Mountain View School stands in 2007, at the junction of North (Maury) and South River. Jordan's furnace had manufactured ordnance for the Mexican War and was called Buena Vista in honor of the American victory at Buena Vista, Mexico. Hart's Bottom and Green Forest were consolidated into a new town called Buena Vista—appropriately named, as the English translation is "beautiful scenery."

A.T. Barclay, president of the new promotional company, must have been a world-class salesman. His name appears as early as 1830 in various Rockbridge enterprises such as local fairs, quarries, and Washington College where he served as trustee.

Barclay knew the importance of history. His first prospectus included a quote from George Washington, who called the area "the garden of America." Barclay expanded the description to take in the entire planet. He referred to Buena Vista as "the mineral center of the world." His friend at the college, noted geologist W.H. Ruffner, was commissioned to write a glowing assessment of available minerals, which were considered to be inexhaustible. Another slight exaggeration is contained in Ruffner's report where he asserted, "The bottom lands are not subject to river overflow to any great extent." With the advantage of hindsight, I wonder if Mr. Ruffner blushes in heaven when he sees his little Utopia submerged in muddy water and designated a federal disaster area.

The lofty claims brought startling, almost frightening success. Barclay toured America, persuading wealthy businessmen to invest in this wonderful location. By February of 1890 he could announce with authority that twenty-two new industries had come to Buena Vista and more were on the way. Proof stood before the eyes of any citizen who cared to climb a nearby hill and take a look. Within a span of two years, more than six hundred new buildings had been constructed, including some very substantial homes and factories facing uncommonly wide city streets. There were three hotels, two restaurants, thirty boarding houses, three wholesale outlets, a hardware store, two stove stores, three churches, one grade school, a female academy, and a large opera house. The busy manufacturing plants were lined up along the river and the railway.

The new city was remarkably self-contained. Iron, mica, granite, slate, limestone, and feldspar were mined on the spot, then trundled only a few blocks to factories that turned out finished products. Timber was harvested within the town limits. Much of it stayed there, processed by the lumber mills. Woodworking shops turned the boards into furniture. Carpenters used the material for construction of homes. Paper mills and tanneries made use of forest byproducts. Saddles, bricks, stoves, stationery, glass, cloth, and wagons were manufactured in town, almost exclusively from raw material gathered within corporate limits. The Rarig Iron and Steel Works located uptown designed and built most of the machinery required by the factories. All of this amazing creativity could be tracked from start to finish without stepping outside the city limits. A busy railway connected this mining/manufacturing metropolis to the world market.

Small wonder that people were eager to buy into the action of "Infant Pittsburgh." The climate was moderate, the scenery was breathtaking, and productivity was unlimited. Rockbridge neighbors elbowed each other in the real estate offices, mortgaging homes and farmland to buy city lots.

A few voices advised caution. The Reverend Dr. Lafferty of Washington College was one of them. After carefully examining the real estate, he noted that the lots were selling at prices comparable to central New York City. There was one major difference, and he spoke of it: crawdads were still building their mud tunnels in Buena Vista. He declined all offers and went back to Lexington's higher ground. Almost everybody agreed that the cautious clergyman was nothing but "an old fogy."

In contrast, the promoter Barclay was definitely not a fogy. His style was upbeat, positive, and popular. His Buena Vista Company flourished. To his credit it must be admitted that he relied on basic honesty. He simply chose not to mention any negative aspects. At the first annual meeting of the company, he could report a surplus of more than one million dollars. Stockholders were delighted. People who had bought expensive lots felt justified and secure.

Then came the terrible economic depression of the 1890s that persisted through the end of the century. All across America factories slowed, then closed. The pain felt in Rockbridge and Buena Vista was no exception. Nevertheless, the town survived. Much of the manufacturing continued, though at a slower pace. Population growth stalled. Interestingly, A.T. Barclay had predicted with great enthusiasm that the population of the city would exceed six thousand inhabitants. It did, but he was off by one hundred years.

The mineral deposits were not quite as huge as projected. The "overflow" of the scenic river proved to be a continuing problem. Yet the floods have not succeeded in driving away the people. Occasional rebuilding is necessary, but commerce continues.

It remains to be seen how the little city will handle changes brought on by the burgeoning Southern Virginia University in its midst. Will the school be perceived as a life-giving asset or a threat? Can the citizens welcome tourism as a growing major industry? One thing is certain: the natural beauty of river and mountain can have strong appeal for tourists. That could not possibly be true if "Infant Pittsburgh" had been allowed to grow to maturity.

Lesson 43:
Lexington's Little Boom

There was nothing quiet about Rockbridge County in the year 1890. The years of scarcity had passed. Sturdy citizens had proven they could rebuild and prevail despite the terrible privations of a civil war. Smooth steel railroads had replaced the bone-rattling stagecoach paths. Passenger trains sped through the area, and freight cars opened far more markets than the canal system, which itself had been something of a miracle for thirty years. Exuberance abounded.

Industrialists from every direction took notice of the clear potential in Rockbridge. After all, the resources of field, forest, river and mine were unrivalled and apparently unlimited. Frank Leslie's *Illustrated Newspaper* of July 1890 had this to say about our Valley:

> The climate is one of the greatest charms. Spring and autumn seasons here are what poets and artists dream of, while summer is fresh with the breeze from mountaintops. Here are mineral and manufacturing resources equal to those of Birmingham, with the water-power of Lowell, the healthful and delightful climate of Asheville, the accessibility of Chattanooga combined with natural beauties and attractions of scenery and location unsurpassed anywhere.

What could possibly prevent economic development in such a paradise? Promoters, on paper, laid off exciting towns at Goshen, Glasgow, Buena Vista, Cornwall, and Springfield (near Natural Bridge). Imposing hotels arose to accommodate the expected flood of wealthy investors. Some of those hotels remained unoccupied, including the one constructed at the junction of Irish Creek and South River (Cornwall).

We examine that unlikely site today and wonder: What were they thinking? They were thinking about getting rich. It seems

odd, totally out of character. Rockbridge had been founded by
Scot-Irish settlers. They instilled in their children the biblical
sweat-of-the-brow work ethic. They insisted that nothing in life
comes easy, if it is to be worthwhile. Worldly pleasures point
toward hell. Rich people could not expect to negotiate the straight
and narrow path to heaven. Suddenly a new concept caught
on. The unfamiliar lure of instant wealth became acceptable.
Conservative Presbyterian farmers, previously known for their
stiff and stern frugality, stormed the land offices, handing over
buckets of cash no one suspected they had. Even the high-energy
salesmen were astonished.

Lexington was slow to catch the fever, much to the consternation
of more than one editor. Local newspapers urged business leaders
to wake up, to promote and sell the town as the "Athens Of The
South." Several prominent citizens took heed, quickly setting
up the Lexington Development Company. Following the pattern
established by Goshen, Cornwall, Buena Vista, and Glasgow,
hundreds of residential and commercial lots were laid off in a
widening circle from the center of Lexington, leaving room for
a sweeping beltway to help with traffic. It strikes me as strange
that although the paper plats were extremely attractive, any
sane citizen could look at the Cornwall and Lexington terrain.
They could see cliffs and ravines where the drawings showed
everything flat. The few voices of reason were publicly scorned.

The *Rockbridge County News* of October 23, 1890, ran this
editorial:

> It is with a feeling of sincere gratification that we
> today record Lexington's great awakening. The
> old town has aroused from her lethargy. She has
> caught the spirit of the times, and is girding up
> her loins to march to the front and take her place
> among the most vigorous and prosperous towns
> of the land. Lexington is the terminus of two trunk
> lines of railroad, the Baltimore and Ohio and the

Chesapeake and Ohio. They use a common track to a Union Depot within the limits of the town. There are six passenger trains daily, giving easy and quick connection to all points East, West, North, and South. The Shenandoah Valley Railroad is reached within eight miles by a rail connection at Buena Vista. The Virginia Western Railroad will be built to a connection with the Tennessee Midland Railroad, thus making a Grand Trunk Road from Lexington, Virginia to Memphis. There is every reason to believe that the Pittsburgh and Glasgow Railroad will soon cross the B&O at Lexington, thus giving a short and direct connection with that great center of iron consumption. The Cumberland Valley Railroad has reached Winchester in its progress up the Valley and is expected to give Lexington its fifth railroad in the very near future. Then will be fulfilled the prediction of John W. Garrett, late president of the B&O, that Lexington, Virginia will become one of the great railroad centers of the South.

It did not happen. The only trains arriving at the Union Depot downtown were forced to back their slow way in from the shared Y at East Lexington. But boom fever spread anyway. The other local newspaper, the *Gazette*, carried dizzying reports of British investors buying into Rockbridge with as much as five million dollars. The Duke and Duchess of Marlborough had purchased lots in Glasgow. A huge steel mill was under construction near the ruins of Liberty Hall just west of the town limits.

The great metropolis did not materialize, except as countless deeds on paper. In the Rockbridge courthouse, Deed Book 76 documents the frenzy. In one short year a worldwide recession put a stop to the flow of money. Disillusioned investors angrily pointed accusing fingers at the Lexington Development Company, most of whom were officers in the local Presbyterian church.

Editors fell strangely silent. The steel mill did not rise to obstruct the view of House Mountain. Its completed foundations were filled in with clay, to become tennis courts for Washington and Lee University. Those playgrounds have now been in use for more than a century and in the opinion of many are more of an asset than a smoking steel mill.

The irrational exuberance of 1890 gave way to a sad pessimism that persisted in Rockbridge for two decades. It would require the fortitude of Pennsylvania lumbermen to restore some hope and health in our county. Their story is the subject of another history lesson, the annals of little Cornwall.

Lesson 44:
A Small Industry Brings Hope to Rockbridge

The economic mood of Rockbridge had plummeted. Exuberance of the 1890s gave way to despair as one boom after another suffered collapse. Morale fell even lower in 1895 when the primary bank had to close because of the dishonesty of its highly esteemed manager. Virtually every household suffered painful financial losses. The situation did not encourage harmony. Bewildered citizens looked at each other and wondered who could be trusted.

When the Whitmer and Steele Lumber Company of Pennsylvania announced plans to build an impressive processing plant at Cornwall, people were understandably dubious. They had seen too many false promises. They had watched a luxury hotel arise on the hilltop during the boom, only to be torn down later as scrap, without serving a single patron. The name of their community had been changed from Crowder to Cornwall with the high expectation that America's only tin mine would soon rival the production of Cornwall, England. However, legal complications had closed the tin mine, and the valuable ore lay undisturbed, as it still does a century later. Yes, the Norfolk and Western Railway was there, but all marketable timber stood in formidable folds of the mountains, seemingly inaccessible.

Before the unbelieving eyes of Rockbridge County, Whitmer and Steele carefully made it happen. First they built eighteen sturdy homes, with a schoolhouse in the center of the village. Workers would occupy those homes, and young students would go to school each day, within sight and sound of their mothers. Two large boarding houses were constructed, then a secure general store, to be leased to a local proprietor. Finally a giant lumber mill, complete with a pond for sorting logs, materialized beside the railroad. Scores of native families were employed, and they were paid on time. The mood began to improve along South River and Irish Creek. These Pennsylvanians obviously knew what they were doing. One question remained: How will those faraway trees ever get to Cornwall?

Whitmer and Steele had done it before, in the gentler terrain of Pennsylvania. They would use a narrow guage mountain railroad to probe the challenging slopes and ravines. They hired a young Rockbridge surveyor, Douglas Brady. He accomplished a task that still seems impossible, the erection of more than fifty-seven miles of steel track in those mountains. Reclusive settlers who thought they had escaped civilization deep in the forested hills watched a railroad come past their cabins. Young people applauded. Old-timers held on to their rifles, wondering whether to move or to fight. The railway penetrated all major hollows on the western slope, and eventually crested the mountain to bring logs to Cornwall from the Amherst County side.

The new industry began successful operation around 1915 and served Rockbridge for twenty-five years. It brought economic revival and optimism when both were so desperately needed. The official name became "The South River Lumber Company Of Cornwall, Virginia." Steady employment was provided for more than two hundred families, even throughout the Great Depression that arrived in late 1929.

The largest tree in Rockbridge forests was the American chestnut. Logs with a diameter of six feet were commonly harvested from the chestnut groves atop mountain peaks. When the catastrophic chestnut blight wiped out the entire species, our county was suddenly deprived of several enormous resources: chestnut lumber, tanbark, and hundreds of tons of nuts, which had fed the animal and human population. Despite the setback, the lumber company at Cornwall survived to its full life expectancy. The mill was dismantled in the 1940s. The steel tracks were pulled up, to be reused elsewhere.

The Cornwall village remained, producing generations of citizens noted for the Whitmer-Steele virtues of honesty and diligence. Level-headed descendants absorbed their remarkable example. They understood clearly how some of the grandiose schemes can evaporate overnight, while the modest venture plods stubbornly forward without fanfare to bring about much good.

The South River Lumber Company overcame the early suspicion and won respect and admiration in Rockbridge. Most of the mountain land was turned over to the United States Department of Agriculture as National Forest and continues to produce timber. The National Park Service erected a display on the Blue Ridge Parkway in recognition of the industry. A short segment of railroad has been restored on Douglas Brady's original grade. The marker tells today's travelers that more than one hundred million board feet of lumber were transported to the mill on such a railway. How much lumber is that? Enough to build at least 70,000 typical three-bedroom homes.

The fifty-seven miles of mountain railroad now serve as fire trails for the U.S. Forest Service. If you are a hiker you can enjoy scenery deep in hardwood forests, far more wild and extensive than the popular Chessie Trail along the old canal. Brooks tumble through gorges, sparkling pure, the habitat of native trout. Wild turkeys, ruffed grouse, deer, and bear thrive in the thickets beside your path. Such is the legacy of a little industry that is now all but forgotten, an industry that replaced gloom with hope when it was needed most.

An interesting side-note: The surveyor Douglas Brady's son Pat married an Oxford girl named Mary Johnston, sister to John William, sitting with us as I present this lesson.

Lesson 45:
The Pettigrew Tragedy

In the graveyard of Oxford Church stands an unusual square monument with inscriptions on all sides. It replaces an earlier stone marker that was destroyed by lightning. Here is the inscription:

> *In memory of a mother and five children who perished in the snowstorm of 17 December 1846 between the two House Mountains. Mary Ann Moore, wife of John Pettigrew, age 41 years and 10 months. Judith Annie, 14 years and 7 months. Margaret Jane, 12 years and 10 months. Letitia Ann, 10 years and 11 months. John Thomas, 8 years and 4 months. Mary Elizabeth, 6 years and 3 months. The husband and father on his return home three days after the sad event was the first to discover that his house was in ashes and his wife and five children were cold in death. John Pettigrew, February 1805– August 8, 1848.*
>
> *This monument was erected by a sympathizing community in 1847. Replaced by the citizens of Collierstown and Buffalo December 1902.*

The grief-stricken father died less than two years after his unspeakable loss. There remained but one survivor...his sixteen-year-old daughter Rachel. Rachel was not at the homestead that terrible night. She was caring for her ailing grandmother on Kerrs Creek, several miles to the north.

Where was John Pettigrew that night? He was at the home of his employer William Alphin, who owned a store and distillery near the foot of Big Hill on the Collierstown side of House Mountain. It was John's routine to walk the rugged two-mile trail to his home only once a week, usually on Sunday, bringing treats and necessities to the eager family. Six days a week, he worked and lodged and worked at the Alphin place. By all accounts John was a man of kindness, integrity, and dependability, always loving and dedicated to his family.

Rachel describes the domestic situation as happy. She remembers the home nestling in that lovely saddle between the landmark peaks of Rockbridge. Their house was not totally isolated. Less than five hundred yards away stood another cabin occupied by James and Mary Anderson. Why did this neighboring couple not sound an immediate alarm? Following the deadly night of fire and storm, could they have been unaware of the catastrophe? We shall never know the answer. However, their silence and their detachment did arouse suspicion.

Poor little Rachel was not finished with tragedy and suffering. In 1846 her mother and siblings died, and two years later she lost her father. In 1855 she married James Reynolds, and exactly two years later her young husband died, leaving Rachel a widow with two tiny daughters, Mary and Sarah. Little Sarah was crippled for life at age five, a victim of rheumatic fever. In spite of such difficulties, mother and daughters survived to old age. Sarah married John Mackey Knick and bore six children, one of whom was Miss Sadie.

I consider myself fortunate to have known Rachel's granddaughter, Miss Sadie Knick. Sadie was a member of Collierstown Presbyterian Church while I was pastor there during the early 1960s. Sadie had listened intently when her grandmother Rachel told her family's story, probably often. Then in 1946 Sadie did something very few people do: she wrote it down. Elizabeth Knick Clark, a later descendant of Rachel, gave me a copy. Most of the information for this history lesson comes from Sadie's document.

Sadie's account of the tragedy indicates a confident belief that murder was involved and that James and Mary Anderson were the perpetrators. Dr. Wilkinson and Dr. Rogers, the two local physicians, determined during an inquest that wounds on the mother's head and neck contributed to her death. There were no marks of violence on the children. A careful search of the ruins found no trace of the household silverware or other valuables, raising the possibility of theft. James and Mary Anderson were eventually brought to trial in Lexington. The jury acquitted Mary but found James guilty of murder. For some reason Judge Lucas Thompson set the guilty verdict aside and ordered that Anderson be tried in Bath County. The second trial acquitted Anderson, to the disgust of the bereaved kinfolk.

Sadie records how the weather on that tragic night was of historic severity. Snow fell to a depth of eighteen inches. The wind howled at gale force, and the temperature fell to ten below zero. Under such extreme conditions, life hangs in the balance. For the sturdy forty-one-year-old mother and her offspring, the balance was tripped, either by man or by nature or both, and they perished. The entire community united in the shock of grief and sympathy.

Visit the Pettigrew plot outside our church door. Say a prayer for the pitiful family, and give thanks that such enormous catastrophe is uncommon in our day.

Note: Descendants of Rachel Pettigrew were in attendance at Oxford Church as this history lesson was presented.

Lesson 46:
Short Hill Turnpike

The twin peaks of House Mountain may be the most commanding feature in Rockbridge County topography today, but Short Hill has more historic impact. Without Short Hill there would be no Natural Bridge. Without Natural Bridge our county would have a different name.

Viewed from the valley floors, there is nothing to indicate that Short Hill is a double mountain with two crests. Old maps are more correct, referring to the mountain in the plural as "Short Hills." Between the two crests lies an upland valley, level and lush. Cedar Creek is up there, beginning as extensive marshland. It flows northward for a mile or two, then falls off the east flank of the mountain and turns due south. For thousands of years Cedar Creek cut through an underground cavern on its way to the James. The roof of that cavern gradually collapsed and washed away, except for the one segment we now call Natural Bridge.

Settlers first chose homesites along the Great Path in the Valley of Virginia, but as others came they found equally fertile land closer to the mountain slopes. Buffalo Creek formed a rich secondary valley just west of the Path. Short Hill separated the two, a seemingly insurmountable barrier. Lumbering bison had found several ways to cross the high ridge walking single file. Settlers followed those paths, knowing that a horse could go wherever buffalo walked.

Where Cedar Creek makes its 180-degree turn southward, one path leads up into the hidden meadows. Another path, slightly to the north, winds up and over the mountain with great determination and then drops down into Buffalo Valley on the other side. Incredibly, that path became a major east-west route connecting today's Glasgow with Clifton Forge. Our Scot-Irish and German ancestors were obviously not intimidated by Short

Hill Mountain. For one hundred years, they chose to push directly over its crest rather than go around it as we do today on the level route.

What was their motivation to use that stony path? The answer lies in one word: trade. Settlers had soon found that these rich valleys could easily produce more than was needed for survival. Surplus could be traded for goods and cash, but transporting the abundance was a serious problem. As early as 1756 George Washington had toured the area. The natural resources impressed him. He cautioned that western Virginia's commerce should not be allowed to flow toward the Mississippi and thus to the Spaniards of New Orleans. His persistent advice was to make use of Virginia's east-flowing rivers. That is precisely what was done.

In Rockbridge, the first major cash crop was hemp, a form of marijuana. It grew in wild profusion and could be manufactured into rope that was in demand worldwide. First packhorses, then eventually wagons crossed the spine of Short Hill, moving the hemp from Buffalo to the James River. By the time of the Revolution, flour and cornmeal were the chief commercial products, explaining the proliferation of water-powered mills on every stream. Thrifty settlers knew that grain could be converted into whiskey, generating a dependable market. Since a jug of whiskey and a wagonload of grain were similar in value, few people had difficulty deciding which product they would tote across the mountain to sell.

By the first quarter of the 1800s, commerce across Short Hill was significant enough to justify a major state road. The Natural Bridge-Clifton Forge Turnpike was chartered. Tolls, taxes, and private investors produced a substantial thirty-five-mile wagon road. Buffalo citizens called their section the Short Hill Turnpike. For one hundred years that colorful mountain road provided access to the world. Imagine the adventure of hauling heavy loads of iron or whiskey up one side, resting at the summit, and then attempting the more difficult task of keeping it under control on the downward slope. At Glasgow boats ran to and from Richmond when the water level was right. George Washington would have been pleased.

A few weeks before writing this lesson, my research prompted me to hike the entire Buffalo portion of the Short Hill Turnpike. In a forest that seems remote, the old road is yet visible. Surprisingly, the grade is not steep. From creek to summit it winds in and out of the hollows with a steady upward consistency. Near the top, strong pioneers carefully placed hundreds of rock slabs to support the downhill edge through difficult terrain. At the crest the road crosses through a narrow gap between enormous rocks.

Try to imagine the scene. For uncounted centuries deer and buffalo knew and used this spot. Indian hunters camped here on their way back to the Ohio country. Settlers lugged their few possessions through this pass to make permanent homes in Buffalo Valley. Reverend Samuel Houston, that near-genius American patriot who ran his farm and academy at Rural Valley, stopped here dozens of times. While pastor at Oxford, Houston earned a reputation for never being late despite snows and forest fires. On this crest he performed marriages, reducing by half the four-hour trip between Buffalo and Rural Valley.

Later the trail became the turnpike, with a sixty-six-foot right of way that I am told is yet owned by the state of Virginia. The actual track was only fourteen feet wide, but it made for successful wheeled commerce. People in stagecoaches rode here on their way to the Blue Grass Trail across the next mountain and on to Kentucky. Heavy wagons loaded with tanbark and leather and charcoal rattled across this rocky ridge. Onyx from Rapps Mill came through here on its way to Richmond and the Atlantic Ocean.

When I hiked back down to South Buffalo I wondered where the tollgates had been placed. How did these frugal people come up with the few cents required for man and horse? Then I remembered reading how dozens of local paths discreetly bypassed the tollhouses, only to connect with the main road farther up the mountain. The practice was so widespread that articulate Buffalo residents coined a new name. Instead of Short Hill Turnpike, they called it Short Hill Shunpike until it went out of business. It is simply not in the nature of the Scot-Irish to pay for something that has been free, especially something as strenuous as crossing Short Hill.

Lesson 47:
Church and State

From state church to voluntary religion: how did we get there? The process was not easy. Few people realize the significant impact made by Rockbridge County citizens throughout the struggle. Virginia began with a government-controlled religion. This was the way of the world—the ruler established the religion of the people. In Scotland the established church was Presbyterian. Here in the colony, the Anglican Church was called the Church of England, the Church of Virginia, and the Established Church. Clergy included bishops, priests, and vicars, some of whom were noble and gifted leaders.

There was no separation of church and state. When a county was established, so too was a parish. The government appointed justices and vestries to watch over the county and keep things orderly. The justices managed criminal behavior, while the vestries looked after social behavior. Vestries ensured that citizens remained morally upright and attended church faithfully. They cared for the indigent and found homes for orphans. Vestries also collected taxes so courthouses and parish churches could be built. Both vestries and justices were paid by order of the government and were considered representatives of the King of England, who at that time was acknowledged Head of the Church. For about 150 years, this religious monopoly worked reasonably well while the colonial population remained east of the mountains.

In the mid 1700s, Virginia's colonial government under Governor Gooch began encouraging Non-Anglicans to come into the colony. It was intended that the Non-Anglicans, or Dissenters, would create a natural buffer between the more English settlements in Eastern Virginia and the French and Indians toward the West. Religious toleration improved. Dissenters came here because land was cheap and because they would not be required to conform to the established church. They soon turned the system on its head by becoming the majority seated on the vestry.

From the beginning of the American experiment, most leaders agreed that the colonies would not survive without the Christian faith. Only the refining influence of the church would and could prevent catastrophic lawlessness. The first settlers sailed mostly from London and they brought their Anglican religion with them. The pastors were Church of England Protestants and deserve our respect. Highly educated, these clergymen provided the only classical libraries and schools in the colonies. By law they were not allowed to be lazy. They were required to produce articulate Christians, young and old. They held Sabbath services without fail. They organized advanced classes as well as primary educational opportunities for all who could afford to pay. Some of them made fervent efforts to Christianize the Indians, until that goal was abandoned as a hopeless cause.

The clergy were part of the government, and there were laws governing civil and moral behavior. If the church was displeased with any citizen who failed to demonstrate proper respect, it could order severe punishments. In some of the colonies, public whipping was the reward for those who could not recite the creeds correctly. Profanity was punished by piercing the offender's tongue. Failure to attend Sabbath worship was considered the ultimate offense. If repeated, the penalties became more life-threatening and could end in public execution. This iron-fisted system was effective. Everybody went to church. To this day there are some who argue that enforced religion was a good thing. They have a name: antidisestablishmentarians, one of the longest words in our language.

Several factors working simultaneously brought on the demise of the state church and "established religion." Public opinion turned against the clergy when they demanded ever-higher salaries. The second factor involved the backlash generated by the established church's prosecution of "dissenting" or non-Anglican preachers. Reverend Alexander Craighead of Borden's Grant was arrested for his Presbyterian preaching and his forceful calls for liberty. His heroic colleagues to the east, Reverend Samuel Davies and Reverend Francis McKemie were also jailed. Several Baptists were held for trial in Spotsylvania.

Fortunately for them, Patrick Henry rode fifty miles from Hanover to volunteer his notable legal assistance. He defended their right to preach. In a fiery speech before the court, the young lawyer went on record and shamed the established church, "Do you mean that in this new land of liberty, good men can be arrested for WHAT? For preaching the gospel of the Son of God? Great God!" His roaring exclamations were repeated, until finally the embarrassed judge shouted an order, "Sheriff, release those men!" The year was 1768, almost a decade before Patrick Henry's "give me liberty or give me death" speech. He turned the tide. Anglican clergy were never happy to have competition. They were understandably reluctant to give up their power. However, they lost. Prosecution of dissenting preachers came to an end.

The heaviest force in dismantling America's establishment of religion came from west of the Blue Ridge. Here is where Scot-Irish and German settlers proved they had no need of England's army or England's church. The Revolutionary War had won political independence for our growing nation, but the established church continued. Patrick Henry had become governor of Virginia and, despite his love of liberty, he was convinced that religion should be supported by tax dollars. Taxpayers could decide which church to support. However, in the tiny village of Lexington, Virginia, a genius sat down and over the course of several summer evenings wrote a document challenging Patrick Henry's position. His name was Reverend William Graham, the Presbyterian rector of Liberty Hall. His argument: "Almighty God does not need government laws nor government dollars. Religion must be left to the voluntary conscience of every individual." Such a concept was new. It was daring. It was untried.

William Graham is perhaps the only man who could have persuaded his Presbytery of Hanover to adopt such a radical document. They did so unanimously and sent it to the Virginia legislature. There Thomas Jefferson helped write it into law, first for Virginia and finally for the nation. Jefferson was so proud of the achievement he ordered it chiseled into his tombstone: "Author of Virginia's Statute For Religious Freedom." Incredible as it may seem today, the successful movement from state church to total religious freedom had its origin here in Rockbridge. It is part of our heritage, largely unrecognized.

The bill was finally passed in 1785. After more than 150 years with an established religion, church and state were separated... almost. Our United States constitution strictly forbids Congress from setting up a state church or prohibiting the free exercise of religion. Nevertheless, Congress does employ government-paid clergy as chaplains of both houses, and every legislative day begins with prayer. Government still retains the power to license pastors for performing religious marriage services. In order to marry, couples obtain a license from the state. Churches are free from taxation, which means that they enjoy some support from the government. Contrary to popular rhetoric, there really is no "wall of separation" between church and state.

Patrick Henry and many others had feared that without state money, churches would disappear and morality would suffer. Freedom of conscience had the opposite effect. Houses of worship flourished and were called "churches," regardless of denomination. Although most of the early schools had been organized and conducted by pastors, general education proved resilient without religious support. People voluntarily professed and chose their faith. They gave financial contributions to their churches, far beyond what had been expected.

Gone forever are the days when a minister of the gospel had the power to spike your tongue or lash your body or end your life. We do well to remember and to thank William Graham for his heroic brilliance. Thank Patrick Henry for offering his unparalleled eloquence in defense of dissenters. Thank Thomas Jefferson for his gifted writing of laws that stand the test of time. Thank God Almighty for the blessings of liberty.

Lesson 48:
Rockbridge Whiskey

Alcohol in Rockbridge has a turbulent history. When our Scot-Irish ancestors settled in the Great Valley, whiskey was considered a necessary staple just as it had been perceived in the Old Countries. Virtually every substantial farm ran a commercial distillery. Some of the buildings stand today, as solid as they were 250 years ago. The beautiful stone structure gracing the front yard of an estate on Kyger Hill is an ancient distillery, a monument to careful construction.

The formal records of New Providence Church indicate that at one time there were eight elders governing the church. Seven of those pious churchmen each owned and operated a commercial whiskey-making operation. Profits from the sale of "adult beverages" helped build a number of churches in Rockbridge, especially Presbyterian houses of worship. Historians assert that the large copper ball on the steeple of Lexington Presbyterian Church had been part of a still. A recent catastrophic fire destroyed that colorful memento to the industry.

Between 1856 and 1900 an annual average of sixty thousand gallons of commercial whiskey was exported from Rockbridge on canal boats alone. Additionally, a nearly equal amount was transported to markets by horse and wagon. When we add in the phenomenal export of iron and flour during those years, it becomes clear that Rockbridge economy was flourishing.

Time brings changes. People were not simply manufacturing alcoholic beverages. They were apparently consuming liquor to such a degree that intemperance became a problem. "Temperance Societies" began to appear. They were motivated to build temperance halls, where regular meetings were held. Most of the members were not advocating temperance...they wanted total abstinence, and they wanted their view to become law. Such a position was radical. It engendered hostility. Questions of morality were entangled with the issue of commerce. On North Buffalo, a temperance hall was built but mysteriously burned to the ground. When rebuilt, it burned again.

Across America the temperance movement spread with astonishing success. Prohibition of alcohol was voted into the United States Constitution but survived only a few years, from 1919 to 1932. During the moral struggle, wine largely disappeared from the sacrament of the Lord's Supper. One outraged Presbyterian elder protested the new style so vigorously his famous quote has been preserved. "When my Saviour asks that I drink a bit of wine in remembrance of Him, ye'll not find me drinking limp grape juice as a substitute."

The Bible has proven to be of limited help on the subject. In several passages strong drink meets with disapproval. In other verses it is described as a gift from God. Jesus drank wine and on one occasion turned some 180 gallons of water into superior wine for the wedding in Cana.

Rockbridge no longer produces a significant amount of whiskey. Wineries, on the other hand, are making an increasing impact on the economy. Attitudes about alcohol continue to vary from person to person and are often held with high passion. Roy Blount, a southern writer, has preserved for us the memorable reply of a politician who was asked to take a stand on the controversial subject. Here is his reply:

> My friends, I had not intended to address this difficult issue at this particular time. However, I want you to know that I do not shun controversy. I will take a stand on any issue at any time. You have asked me how I feel about whiskey. All right, here is how I feel about whiskey. If when you say 'whiskey' you mean the devil's brew, the poison scourge, the bloody monster that defiles innocence, dethrones reason, destroys the home, creates misery and poverty, yea takes the bread from the mouths of children; if you

mean the evil drink that topples Christian men and women from the pinnacle of righteous, gracious living into the bottomless pit of degradation and despair and shame and helplessness and hopelessness, then certainly I am against it.

But if when you say 'whiskey' you mean the oil of conversation, the philosophic wine, the ale that is consumed when good fellows get together, that puts a song in their hearts and laughter on their lips and the warm glow of contentment in their eyes; if you mean Christmas cheer, if you mean the stimulating drink that puts the spring into an old gentleman's step on a frosty crispy morning, if you mean the drink that enables man to magnify his joy and his happiness and to forget if only for a little while life's great tragedies and heartaches and sorrows, if you mean the drink the sale of which pours into our treasuries untold millions of dollars which are used to provide tender care for our little crippled children, our blind, our deaf, our dumb, our pitiful aged and infirm, then certainly I am for it. This is my stand. I will not retreat from it. I will not compromise.

The polititian won the election.

Lesson 49:
Bill Leech, a Christian Gentleman

When you exit the front door of Oxford Church, you are facing Buffalo Creek and majestic Short Hill Mountain, a setting of extraordinary natural beauty. In the center of that pastoral scene, a classic stone house was carefully erected some 230 years ago. The structure has been well maintained and is in excellent condition to this day in 2008. The Leech family, famed for breeding and selling prize Hereford cattle, has owned the property since 1869. On January 19, 2008, William McMasters Leech died, exactly two years after the death of his wife Ruth Morrison. The stone house was their home for the past half-century.

During the previous summer, Bill was honored for his exemplary leadership in the local electrical cooperative. Two of his grandchildren, Holly and Jacob, wrote a tribute for the occasion. They could not have known that six months later their grandfather would be gone. Here is what they wrote:

> Bill Leech: a father of three, loving grandfather of six, and a great grandfather; a farmer, a business man, an active member of his community; a history buff, a poet, an avid reader and chess player, a gardener and lover of all nature...There are so many ways to describe him and so many stories to tell about Bill Leech, it is hard to know where to begin.
>
> He is someone who picked flowers almost every morning for his wife, Ruth. He taught his oldest grandsons to play chess and taught his granddaughter how to ride horses. When his children were young, he lived for snow days when he would manage to come up with an excuse to get in the car and drive into town, no matter how deep the snow, looking for an adventure...all this before four-wheel drive!

He coached his sons' little league teams. He taught Sunday School at his church and continues to be loved and respected by many whose lives he touched when serving in those roles.

He was a doting husband for fifty-five years. He is a wise and gentle father and grandfather to whom his family members go for advice and comfort. He is the first man in his family ever to be a great grandfather.

Many of the Leech family's most cherished stories about Bill include some of the farm animals that he has raised over the years. Bill took great pride in his famed Hereford cattle, but it has been the farm's horses that often conspired to train their trainer and provide entertainment for the entire family, at Bill's expense.

Sam, one of the more stubborn of the work horses, had the duty of plowing the garden. Sam was well trained to take commands to turn left or right, based on specific signals. On days that Sam did not feel like plowing, he would go left when Bill signaled for him to go right, stepping on as many potatoes as he could, to convince Bill to let him off the hook and return to his paddock. Sam usually won the battle!

Headstrong farm animals with minimal work ethic have continued through the generations in the Leech family. April, who is the granddaughter's horse, has also worked diligently to wrap Bill around her hoof. When Holly, the granddaughter, went off to college leaving her horse behind, Bill decided he would ride April to give her much-needed exercise. Sometimes, moments after being saddled and ridden only a short distance, April would trot directly to Ruth and push her soft nose into Ruth's chest, clearly saying, "Make him get off me!" April, now in her late twenties, has retired to her paddock next to Bill's house. She has taken to calling out to him each time he walks out his door. She wants him to come and visit her, bringing mints, as he does every day.

As a testament to his good nature, Bill sought a diplomatic solution when confronted with multiple rabbits taking residence just beyond his beloved garden. Bill's impressive collection of vegetables was always complemented by Ruth's beautiful flowers. Such a wealth of taste was certain to draw family and neighbors. Bill has always been happy to accommodate, letting no visitor leave empty handed. And so, when faced with hungry rabbits eager to help themselves without permission, Bill used his unique problem solving skills to meet the challenge. Rather than disposing of the thieves, as many would have been inclined to do, he planted a section just for the rabbits, then fortified the rest. The unspoken deal was understood by all parties and bloodshed was averted. As recently as last winter Bill constructed a small domicile for a stray rabbit who had sought shelter from the cold in his barn. Such actions have helped to teach valuable lessons in kindness and humaneness to his grandchildren, who are forever grateful.

Above and beyond the rigorous and sometimes comical adventures of farm life, Bill's commitment has revolved around his family. His home has for years been the hub of extended family gatherings and cherished memories. Afternoon swims, building stone dams in Buffalo Creek, horseback riding and exciting ball games were climaxed by memorable country meals from the ancient kitchen.

The fondest memories of his children, nieces and nephews, and grandchildren are of the times spent visiting and taking in the beautiful view from his front porch. A continued daily ritual, you can most often find Bill rocking there in the evening, watching cattle wade in the creek and deer grazing in the fields just below Short Hill, and of course listening to April's frantic nickering reminding him that she has not had her mint!

(Written by Holly and Jacob Leech, June 2007.)

Lesson 50:
In a Mysterious Way

This lesson deals with some unusual incidents in my own ministry. We may pride ourselves on our science and our technology, but there are quite a few areas that still contain mystery.

I had been pastor of the downtown church in Culpeper, Virginia, for several years when Barbara called my office. In obvious distress she declared that something dangerous was about to fall in the main sanctuary. She was having repeated visions of the destruction. "Please go up in the attic and make an inspection," she pleaded. Convinced that I was dealing with an eccentric, I tried to calm her fears, then hung up the phone and went back to my work. The next day Barbara called my wife saying, "I don't think Rev. Douty believes me. Please use your influence." However, I still did not believe Barbara's visions.

Two weeks later my secretary called me while I was at lunch. In an urgent voice she said, "I think you should come to the church. Something weird is happening." It was a windy winter afternoon. I arrived only a few moments before the entire sanctuary ceiling assembly fell in one tangled mass twenty-two feet to the pews below. Engineers finally concluded that wind turbulence swirling through the bell tower and attic had somehow sucked the ceiling upward, breaking supports and allowing total collapse. No inspection could have foreseen the catastrophe, but Barbara had. Fortunately there were no injuries except for a few cuts and bruises sustained by contractors clearing eighteen tons of debris from the sanctuary.

A happier ending came out of my next story. A young mother sat in my office. She needed immediate financial help to avoid eviction from her modest apartment. We agreed that sixty dollars would forestall the threat at least long enough for her to look for a better solution. I wrote her a check for that amount, knowing that I would have to scrape up a deposit to cover it. The day's mail was delivered to my desk as I said goodbye to the woman. When I opened the top envelope, a note inside read: "Reverend Douty, please use the enclosed check in your work with the poor." The check was for exactly sixty dollars. I thanked God, stepped across the street and made the deposit. Coincidence? Maybe.

A similar event happened quite recently but at a different church. For Thanksgiving, the congregation had adopted a poor family. I volunteered to donate the turkey, which would top off the big basket of food. I promised to have it ready for delivery that Sunday immediately after the close of worship. As the congregation filed out that day, Linda whispered in my ear: "I'm delivering the basket. Where is the turkey?" You guessed it. I had completely forgotten that this was the day.

Linda showed some impatience. She was in a bad spot, and her mood reflected it. She had made a promise to the expectant family, and I had let her down. While she was scolding me, I opened the front door. I needed to escape and try to find a turkey. There on the front step stood a strong young man with a huge turkey in each hand. "Our civic club had these left over. Can you use them?" I promptly took one, handed it to Linda, who was not only dumbfounded but also obviously disappointed at being cheated out of her opportunity to hammer me. I put the other bird in the church's freezer, breathing silently, "Thank You God." Coincidence? Perhaps.

Throughout my ministry many small miracles have taken place, enough to fill a book. I will recount only one more. It has significance for Oxford Church, because it involves Charlie Potter. His home is at the back door of our church, although I did not know that at the time. I had bought more than a dozen timbers, each twenty-two feet long. I needed them at my home farm near Timber Ridge. There they lay in Culpeper, at a construction site more than a hundred miles from Rockbridge. They had to be moved immediately. I made urgent phone calls, trying to rent a truck. No suitable equipment was to be found. All the rental trucks were designed to move furniture, not several tons of over-length six by sixes. Time was running out. In the midst of my frustration, Charlie Potter called. I knew him, but for twenty years or more had had no contact with him.

I could not believe my ears when Charlie said, "An equipment company in Culpeper has installed a bed on my new truck. My problem is that I have no convenient way to get it to Rockbridge. Do you ever come this way, and could you possibly drive it down here?" I assured him that I could, tomorrow. Before ending the call, I asked, "By the way Charlie, how long is the cargo bed on this truck?" Quickly came his cheerful reply, "Twenty-two feet." Coincidence? You decide.

My own conclusion is summed up in the words of a favorite hymn:

> *God moves in a mysterious way*
> *His wonders to perform.*
> *He plants His footsteps in the sea,*
> *and rides upon the storm.*

Lesson 51:
Oxford's Academy of Higher Learning

People who comprise the congregation of Oxford Presbyterian Church have inherited a surprising responsibility. They alone have the final word with regard to two acres of real estate now known as "Palmer Community Center." The chain of events that resulted in this situation forms a story worth remembering.

In the year 1902 an unusually gifted Scotsman became pastor of Oxford Church. His name was Reverend Thomas Mowbray. Eighteen months later he had resigned and moved away. Why? His pastor's heart had taken precedence over clear thinking and compelled him to visit a nearby home where the patient lay dying of diphtheria. Mowbray was violating civil law, since the house was plainly marked with the vivid yellow banner of quarantine. One of the pastor's own church officers had the unpleasant task of making the arrest. Oxford Church trembled through eight weeks of controversy, neighbor angrily debating with neighbor over how to treat the preacher who had been so effective in the community. Reverend Mowbray knew he must leave for the sake of church tranquility. The ordeal was heartbreaking. His wife and children loved the brand-new pastor's home, the manse that stood beside the musical Buffalo Creek. They loved the beautiful green meadows and the sheltering peak of Short Hill Mountain. They loved the people of Oxford. It was a tough time for the church.

Despite the brevity of a pastorate begun with such great promise and high hope, Pastor Mowbray left a legacy on Buffalo. It was called "Palmer Academy," soon to become the very first public high school in the county. Reverend Mowbray wanted his children and others to be prepared for college. The small local schools were amazingly productive, but limited to elementary level. Fortunately, one of Oxford's elders, Sidney Saville, shared the Scotsman's vision and was in a position to help make it happen.

Saville had recently served as the Superintendent of Rockbridge Public Schools. He knew how to operate an educational system. Mowbray arrived in March of 1902, and by August he had procured a legal charter, complete with corporate officers and a board of directors approved by the state. Organizational meetings were held here in our church. Rapid progress marked the movement, but there were some protests. A few pious Presbyterians insisted that the house of God is desecrated by secular pursuits such as public education. Eventually they were persuaded to let the good work continue. Six Oxford elders comprised the Board of Directors. Sidney Saville was president, and Reverend Mowbray was secretary-treasurer. A beloved physician, Dr. H.R. Coleman, also signed the application and gave support. One year later, in September 1903, Palmer Academy was standing and ready for use, a mile upstream from Oxford Church and almost in sight of the new church manse, which the charter designated as the corporate office.

That breathtaking project astonished Rockbridge County. Newspaper articles hailed it as a unique institution, nestled in the most lovely and fertile spot on earth. Support had come from the entire Buffalo community, whether the people belonged to Oxford Church or not. Washington and Lee University, through its inspiring president Dr. Robert Denney and other faculty members, gave enormous moral encouragement. A substantial cash donation came from the Honorable Robert Fulton Cutting of New York. Dedication Day offered perfect autumn weather. People flocked past Oxford and the manse to see for themselves the first rural high school in Rockbridge County. Livery stables in Lexington contributed reduced rates for the carriage rides into the country. The celebration proved to be a splendid occasion topped off with the real drawing card: a bountiful meal prepared by Buffalo community women. Their culinary skill has always been noteworthy. It must have been healthy food as well. In dozens of photographs from the 1900s, I see row upon row of remarkably slender, attractive people, male and female, old and young.

A Presbyterian clergyman named Joseph Graves was hired as administrator and principal of the new school. Alas, he did not understand rural discipline. The students apparently took charge. The gentle parson was forced to resign after only one school quarter. Sidney Saville stepped in as manager and teacher, and he quickly won respect. He brought order that proved to be permanent. Both preachers were gone, Mowbray the founder and Graves the first principal. But the school survived, offering classical education for all ages, open to any who could pay the modest tuition. By 1906 the independent days were finished. Our public school system was in place, and Palmer Academy relinquished control to the Rockbridge County Board of Education. In 1907 there were seventy-four children enrolled in ten grade levels. Every teacher was required to give "moral instruction" along with academic studies. Political correctness had not yet been heard of.

As schools consolidated, Palmer became an elementary unit. Higher grades were moved to what is now Effinger. By 1956 the school board closed Palmer. More than one thousand local children had been taught there, and by all accounts, taught well. Some of those students are part of our congregation today. Another generous Oxford Presbyterian, John Swink, stepped forward and bought out the board of education's equity single-handedly so that the well-built schoolhouse could continue as a community center, which it does to this day.

Although Oxford Church holds the deed, and legal documents show that our congregation's opinion controls the destiny of Palmer, it is quite clear that the center is a neighborhood project. Buffalo citizenry cooperate to keep the property alive and well. Able leaders step forward every time a need arises.

When people attend the ice cream suppers or the Christmas celebrations at Palmer, they have fun. It is a happy place. I encourage you to read Clinton Anderson's delightful book entitled *Palmer: The first hundred years in the Buffalo Community*. On the back cover you will find these words: "With God's blessing,

Palmer will continue to foster good fellowship and community service for many years to come."

Where did the name come from? Benjamin Palmer was another Presbyterian pastor, naturally. Sidney Saville heard him preach once at a Washington and Lee commencement. It is the irony of history that a man living in New Orleans who never heard of Buffalo or Palmer Academy should have a school named in his honor. It says to me: Never underestimate the power of a Presbyterian sermon.

Formerly Palmer Academy, Palmer High School, and Palmer Grade School.
Since 1956, Palmer Community Center. Photo 2008.

Lesson 52:
George Diehl and His Buffalo Girl

D r. George West Diehl was pastor of Oxford Church from 1948 to 1967. Iva was the one who brought him to Oxford. She grew up right here on the banks of Buffalo Creek. Iva met and married George, and her life never slowed from that moment. Over the course of a very fruitful half-century the pair lived in various states, but in 1948 Iva came home. She brought her husband with her. Both of them lived the remainder of their lives near the spot where her life began, a few miles upstream from Oxford Church.

George Diehl was born into a Pennsylvania family who moved to the coalfields of West Virginia while he was quite young. When they moved again, to Burkeville, Virginia, George was able to attend Hampden Sydney College for two years. By 1910 he needed a job in order to finance his continuing education. That necessity brought him for the first time to Rockbridge County, where he became a teacher in the Brownsburg public school. By 1913 George had passed two significant milestones. He had graduated from Washington and Lee University, and he had proposed marriage to Iva Shafer whom he had met at a Presbyterian church party. Four years later, he had graduated twice more: from Union Theological Seminary with a degree in religion and from the University of Richmond with a master's degree in English.

George and Iva were married during the turbulent years of World War I. George was employed in a small mission school at Grundy, Virginia, for three years. Then the couple moved to the familiar coalfields of West Virginia where George served as school superintendent for two years. His work so impressed the state education officials that they offered him the president's position at Concord State College. He accepted. Iva attended the college and earned a bachelor's degree there. Then she became Dean of Women for Concord.

George Diehl assumed the presidency of Morris Harvey College in Barboursville, West Virginia. It was he who recommended the relocation of the college to Charleston, West Virginia. The move was eventually made, but only after George had gone to the University of Chicago for graduate studies. Meanwhile, Iva had become Dean of Women at Elon College in North Carolina. Both were happy when George accepted a position as pastor in Dallas, Texas, and their lives were reunited once more at the same address. They were in Dallas only three months before George accepted a call to be pastor of the First Presbyterian Church of Corpus Christi. This time, they put down roots. The Diehls remained in Corpus Christi for seventeen years, both of them enjoying immensely productive lives. Under George's leadership, the church grew to a membership of nearly two thousand. Iva became Professor of Bible and Dean of Women at Del Mar College.

By 1948 George and Iva were ready for retirement. They moved to her homeplace on the creek in Rockbridge, but retirement eluded them. Dr. Diehl became pastor of Oxford Church without a pause. He preached his last sermon in Texas the end of May and his first sermon in Oxford the beginning of June. Iva managed the massive restoration of the home, including construction of two new wings. They bought out the surviving heirs of two properties, which increased their total real estate to 850 acres. Some of the land extended across the summit of Short Hill and down the other side to Cedar Creek, the stream that created the Natural Bridge of Virginia.

The Diehls chose an attractive name for their property. Iva's middle name was Dunn. They at first called the place "Dunn-Diehl," but it sounded too much like the close of a bargain (done deal), so they shortened the name to Dundee. For more than a half-century Dundee Plantation has been something of a showplace on Buffalo. George and Iva were childless, but they provided a foster home for a small West Virginia boy named Charles Zink. They raised him as their own son to adulthood. Charles and his wife inherited Dundee Plantation and lived there after retirement.

Church records show that George and Iva's influence was enormous. The congregation grew. Dr. Diehl did not confine his work to Oxford Church. He was immediately elected president of the Rockbridge Historical Society. He wrote weekly columns for local newspapers. He published several books. He became a genealogist of national fame. Dr. Diehl is recognized today as a leading authority on Virginia's history. All of this he accomplished after his first "retirement"! At age eighty he retired again, closing his ministry at Oxford but continuing work as interim pastor of Timber Ridge Associate Reformed Presbyterian Church. When he died suddenly in August 1975, Dr. Diehl had been pastor of Oxford for nearly nineteen years and pastor of Timber Ridge an additional seven years.

Iva had died in 1965. Charles Zink and his wife Joanna moved to Dundee from Nebraska. They took over management of the farm and provided domestic care for Dr. Diehl and Iva's sister Lillian who also lived at Dundee during the final years of her life. Charles and Joanna inherited all the property. They were particularly active in the life of Oxford Church for fifteen more years.

George and Iva Diehl left quite a legacy in West Virginia, Texas, and Virginia. They were ultimate "achievers," as described in *Rural Virginia Magazine* issued from Richmond, Virginia, in February 1961. One surviving nephew sits in this congregation today as I present their history. His name: John William Johnston, whose mother Lora Shafer was Iva Diehl's sister. John bears gracefully a heritage that by any standard must be intimidating.

Lesson 53:
What is the Lord's Song?

Congregational singing in Rockbridge has a fascinating and turbulent history. Some of our prominent houses of worship owe their existence to the fiery controversy over what songs are proper. Devout churchmen knew that the Bible commands God's people to come before His presence with singing. They could not agree on the finer point of what songs God really wants or approves. For the hundred years between 1650 and 1750, the Westminster Confession had allowed biblical passages to be sung in worship. However, the ritual bore little resemblance to congregational singing as we know it today.

In those early years of Rockbridge, all the churches were Presbyterian but were known as meeting-houses since only the state religion could be called a church. The typical meeting-house had two pulpits, one for the preacher and one for the precentor. The preaching pulpit stood high up, close to the rafters. The precentor's perch was only half as high. The precentor or prechanter would sing or chant a line from one of the Old Testament psalms, to be repeated by the congregation until the entire passage was completed. The "lining out" method was so repetitious it enabled worshippers to memorize whole chapters of the Bible. Most churches covered the entire book of the Psalms in one year.

The resulting sound could hardly be called "music." Comments found in any number of historic sources give us a rather dismal picture. Every worshipper was obligated to join in, even if the effort was out of tune and out of time. Some writers described the song as whining and droning. Others likened it to the sounds of battle. Words such as "miserable," "quavering," and "discordant" define the singing. One harsh critic bluntly stated that the Presbyterians were obviously trying to imitate the braying of asses. Most surprising is the fact that many of our ancestors honestly believed that this is how things should be in church. To them anything pleasant, whether sound or color or mood, was suspect, and to sing with unison of pitch or rhythm smacked of pomp and ceremony.

After the Revolutionary War one of Rockbridge's most legendary leaders succeeded in bringing about a transformation. He was reverend William Graham, rector of Washington College and pastor of several local Presbyterian congregations. He was not afraid of lively rhythm and melody. As leader of the Liberty Hall militia Graham had observed how soldiers could be motivated and inspired by fife and song. Why not bring that same power into the service of God?

The patriotic hymns of Isaac Watts had played a part in the American Revolution. Both the words and the tunes were easily memorized. Their message appealed to human emotion. However, Watts did not confine his songs exclusively to scripture and that proved to be a problem for conservative Presbyterians in the Valley of Virginia.

William Graham was ahead of his time. He introduced the radical music of Watts wherever he was invited to preach. On more than one occasion such bravado caused many in the congregation to walk out, never to return. They clung to the old way of using psalms, convinced that anything different was sacrilegious. It was their God-given duty to keep the faith pure from dangerous innovation. The new tunes were obviously far too sensual. Anyone could see that they evoked bodily movements, rhythmic swaying, and even tapping of feet. Those who perceived the new trend as evil defiantly allied themselves with other conservative Presbyterians, splitting congregations. Passionate disagreement over such issues created separate Presbyterian churches in Rockbridge, sometimes within sight of each other. The passage of time has softened the once-explosive debate over the Lord's song. Two hundred years later the visitor finds the music in both camps so similar as to be virtually indistinguishable.

William Graham demonstrated his crusading spirit by persuading the first professional music teacher to come to Rockbridge from Connecticut. The musician was Lucius Chapin. He arrived here in 1788 and began teaching the stiff Presbyterians how to sing actual tunes. Within ten years he was able to introduce four-part harmony to hymn singing. The sound was pleasing to human ears, but was it too ornamental for the worship of God? The question has not gone away, but as usual Graham's position ultimately came out the winner.

One wonders why the influence of William Graham is such a well-kept secret in Rockbridge. Few people today have heard of him, yet what he accomplished is astounding. In spite of opposition from every quarter, he conceived and nurtured the school now known as Washington and Lee University. He wrote a document that helped bring about freedom of religion in our nation. He established a theological seminary in Lexington and persuaded the father of our country, George Washington, to be a sponsor. He brought improvements in church music, which remains unchanged across the south to this day. Graham took a Rockbridge native named Archibald Alexander as his student and so inspired the young man that he moved on to create Princeton Theological Seminary. Alexander also absorbed Graham's interest in church music. In 1831 he published one of the most popular hymnbooks ever used in America. It contained more than seven hundred lively songs, many of which are still in use today.

All those who enjoy the melodious tunes and moving words of current church music owe a debt of gratitude to William Graham. It was he who opened the door. Unfortunately, for all his brilliance Graham never chose to follow the biblical advice about soft answers turning away wrath. He won admiration but not affection. He lies alone on the campus of his college, which gave employment some years later to a hero widely known for his soft answers, General Robert E. Lee. For more than a century an endless stream of visitors have come to the site. Are they there to honor the founder? No, they pass by the grave of that genius to place flowers at the resting place of General Lee's horse. Such is the irony of history.

Lesson 54:
Remembering Charlotte Bowyer

We've been told that all is fair in love and war. Don't believe it. There is nothing fair about the treatment of the Bowyer family during the American Civil War.

Beneath the clump of dogwoods in Oxford cemetery stands a neat white tombstone, easily noticed because it stands alone. The inscription reads: "Charlotte Bowyer, wife of Adam Bowyer, died December 8, 1884, age 71 years, gone but not forgotten." She was born in 1811, which means that she was actually 73 years of age. Her plot is large enough to accommodate many more burials. Where is her husband? Why does she lie here alone? I have been given some of the answers. Here is Charlotte's story.

Charlotte's father, Thomas Malone, came across the ocean from Ireland. He married Mary Brown and they settled in Botetourt County, Virginia. Little Charlotte was less than one year old when her father went off to fight in the War of 1812. Thomas came out of the conflict unscathed, only to drown in the Jackson River a few years later. That was the first tragedy in Charlotte's life. She and her mother Mary proved to be strong women, however. The widowed mother Malone lived to be 100 years old.

Charlotte was 21 years of age when she married a young Bedford man of German descent named Adam Bowyer. He was a miller by trade. They had no children for the first seven years, but in 1839 daughter Rebecca was born. Two years later the first son appeared, James Robert. Every other year brought another child, seven in all. We can only guess, but those years must have been the best time in Charlotte's life. From all indications the busy family operated water-powered mills in the Natural Bridge area, perhaps on Broad Creek not far from Oxford Church.

Then came the devastating war between north and south. Life changed drastically for Adam and Charlotte. For reasons not recorded, Adam and James Robert were seized by Union troops and taken away by force. Somehow Charlotte managed to keep her family together even though the protectors and the breadwinners were gone.

We know that mills were a prime target during the Civil War. Both sides understood that a land is weakened when the millers are exiled. Adam and Robert were not soldiers. They were not interested in killing. To the contrary, their profession provided life and food. But it was enough to land them in military custody. Charlotte moved her brood into Upshur County, West Virginia, but even there they were not safe. One of her daughters, Mary Frances nicknamed "Molly" has written of their terror whenever Yankee soldiers appeared. The children were called "little rebels," a term that was no doubt accurate. Watching their father and brother torn from them by heavily armed federal soldiers had understandably turned them into southern rebels forever. The next oldest son Hugh kissed his mother goodbye and angrily enlisted in the confederate army, quickly winning distinction as a brave and gallant soldier.

One day there came a surge of hope. Some well-dressed strangers from the north came into the village, looking for a Mrs. Adam Bowyer. They brought good tidings. Adam and Robert were alive and well, they said. The two prisoners were being held in Fort Delaware, New Jersey. They could be released if adequate payment were made to the federal government, presumably for expenses incurred in their care.

The amount of cash required was staggering. Charlotte and her family, which then included grandmother Bowyer, were willing to do everything in their power to bring home father and son. They sold property and belongings. Becky was grown. Martha and Molly were teenagers. They all contributed everything they could scrape together, sold it, and gave the cash to the federal agents. Although it reduced the family to poverty, they would soon be able to make a fresh start when Adam and Robert returned.

The next part of Charlotte's story will break your heart. The strangers were not federal agents at all. They were slimy carpetbaggers, scam artists who were experts at their profession. They knew that Adam and Robert had both died of typhoid fever in the prison camp. They took advantage of the blind hope ever found in mothers' hearts. Poor Charlotte had gathered the three generations about her every evening as they prayed for restoration: "Please God, let Daddy and Jim-Bob come home." It didn't happen. We do not know how long that family waited with daily expectation, maybe two years, clinging to liars' promises. The war was probably over before the tragic truth came out. My feeling is that there must be a special section of hell reserved for human vultures who prey on grieving widows and orphans.

Charlotte took a deep breath. She had watched her own mother and mother-in-law survive as widows. She would have to do the same. She was past fifty now, but her children were healthy. Hugh was married but had taken his wife with him to Nebraska. Molly turned out to be Charlotte's mainstay. By 1878 Molly had married David Henry Swartz of Augusta County, Virginia. The couple moved back to Rockbridge, apparently bringing mother Charlotte with them. We know that several of Molly's seven children were born at Zollman's Mill, downstream from Oxford Church. While Molly was living there, Charlotte died.

The decision was made to purchase a plot in Oxford cemetery, large enough for several generations. But the Swartz family soon moved a few miles south to Gilmore Mills. No other clan member would join Charlotte at Oxford, even though Molly's last child died a few years later, aged one month.

Descendants of Molly and David Swartz can today be found all over the eastern United States. Their youngest surviving son David Jr. married Minnie Pauline Booze. David and Minnie's third child was a daughter they named Pauline after her mother. The girl came to be called "Polly" by everyone except her immediate family. Polly is in this room with us today, June 1, 2008. She is a clear example of the incredible genetics contributed by her great-grandmother Charlotte. Polly grew up in Buchanan, Virginia.

She married Dr. Edward Turner, late professor of Physics at Washington and Lee University.

One last note of Charlotte's story brings a surprise that proves just how small is our world. Dr. Turner's aunt Bertie Baker is my wife Ellen Baker Douty's grandmother! Amazing Oxford connections never cease.

Lesson 55:
The Missionary from Buffalo

In the year 1925 a young couple stood at the front of Oxford Church and listened as the Reverend Newton Parker spoke those moving words, "I now pronounce you man and wife." The sweet and lovely bride, Ida Saville, had been born and raised near Oxford. Ida's parents had both died in 1907 when she was a toddler. Aunt Estie Saville took her into the home next door on Spring Branch Road. A few years later Ida moved to the home of another relative in Dry Hollow. Her uncle Robert Lucian Saville and his wife Annie Lee Hotinger Saville cared for Ida through the remainder of her childhood. Robert was the brother of Ida's deceased father John.

Ida graduated from Palmer while it still functioned as the local high school. Even though her parents were gone, the extended family recognized the girl's capabilities. Both Ida and her cousin Florence Jane Saville were able to attend college. Both completed their undergraduate work at Harrisonburg State Normal School, now known as James Madison University.

Cousin Florence married Nelson Anderson and remained in the Oxford community, raising one son whom they named Clinton. Today we know him as Dr. Clinton Anderson, a member of our congregation, sitting here with us in the church of his ancestors.

Ida's marriage to Ralph Erskine Moore from Raphine took her to the other side of planet Earth. The young groom, a member of Old Providence Associate Reformed Presbyterian Church, had listened intently to a missionary from India explaining the pressing needs in that far land. A number of Muslims had been converted to Christianity. Through the influence of dedicated Americans, those new Christians were allowed to establish their own communities where each family received a twenty-five acre plot of land which was mostly desert. They desperately needed someone to show them how to grow enough food for survival.

Ralph felt his heart and soul responding, "I am young and healthy. I have two degrees in agriculture. Ida is capable and well educated. Why not answer the call?" They did. Ralph and his bride moved to the mission field in India only three months after their Oxford wedding. They had the support and blessing of both local churches, Oxford and Old Providence.

The remarkable couple accomplished miracles in India despite severe hardship. They made the desert blossom. Ralph showed men and boys how to plant thousands of trees along the canals. He introduced new crops and new ways of growing, using the canal waters for irrigation. Ida taught skills in homemaking, food preservation, and sanitation. She bore her first two children there, and became a living example for child care in a place where infant mortality had long been accepted as inevitable.

Even these challenges were not enough. Ralph and Ida built churches. He had acquired experience in brick-making as well as agriculture. While he and his growing family lived part of the time in a small tent, they built strong Christian churches that stand to this day in what is now Pakistan.

When their term of service ended, Ralph and Ida came home to America during the Great Depression of the 1930s. They stayed in close contact with their friends in India. When their third child, Ralph Jr., became an orthopedic surgeon, he volunteered his skill and his time at the mission hospital in Sahiwal where his parents had served. Dr. Moore was impressed by the love so many of the natives still felt for his parents. Later his own son, Dr. William Moore, followed in the steps of his parents and grandparents, choosing to spend some of his years working in the same Christian hospital.

Today that hospital boasts a School of Nursing heavily supported by the Moore Scholarship Fund. All three generations of Ida's family were concerned with the plight of young women in the Muslim country. To be trained as a nurse invariably gave a girl her ticket to a much better life. The Moore family, through the continuing scholarship fund, has helped hundreds of young women fulfill their dreams. It is happening today. Oxford Church makes a modest contribution to the cause, in honor of Ida Saville, daughter of the church.

Ralph and Ida managed our denomination's Children's Home in Lynchburg, Virginia, for years, then moved to Tennessee and continued the same work for other Presbyterian orphanages. Ralph died in 1972. Ida lived three more years, dying in 1975.

When I speak and write about our local heroes, Ralph and Ida are near the top of the list. Time after time, the Buffalo community has produced remarkable leaders, and Ida is one of them. She and her new husband were willing to leave our beautiful valley flowing with milk and honey. To the glory of God they gave everything, in order to turn a foreign desert into a garden...and they succeeded. Upon returning to their homeland they spent the remainder of their lives serving as model parents for untold scores of troubled children. Furthermore, they passed on their amazing personal commitment. Their children and their children's children inherited and then proved the same dedication.

Such uncommon achievement deserves honor without end. Ida Saville Moore, Oxford's missionary, made a difference. From the peaceful meadows of Buffalo she moved across the world to bring life and hope where she saw the greatest need. She helped build bridges between Muslims and Christians, so necessary for world peace in our own time. She enriched our lives and our heritage with her presence. Our hearts are inspired on this summer morning as we reflect and remember: Ida began right here.

Lesson 56:
Music Makers and More

Some kind of mysterious power pervades Upper Buffalo. The area looks similar to other charming scenes in Rockbridge, but something is different. The little valley has produced uncommonly creative characters in numbers out of all proportion to the population.

Trace the history. Upstream you will find Matthias Rapp tinkering with turbines. He ultimately invented a horizontal water wheel so powerful it could drive his mill with multiple operations. That commercial innovation gave the community a name to put on our map. Only a couple miles downstream is Uncle Bob Hamilton living with gusto and telling tall tales that make people laugh for a hundred years and more. It was he who named the valley "Snakefoot." Other people spoke of his little log church as "Hamilton's School." He called it "Coonskin College." Uncle Bob's daughter Narcissa dared to defy tradition. She became one of the first female leaders in Virginia's educational history. Move a bit farther downstream to find the ghosts of Judge Snakefoot Johnston, Sidney Saville, and Granville Campbell, all of them giants, all of them making history. And there is Palmer Academy, another first in higher education.

Obviously there is a force at work, invisible but persistent. At Spring Branch Road it is amazingly alive today, driving the souls of John and Diana Schofield. Their homestead may look ordinary, but it is not. Inventive genius is thriving there.

The couple came here from Montana a quarter-century ago. John is an environmental engineer with Virginia's Department Of Health. Diana owns and operates a music store in Lexington. Those vocations alone would occupy the full time of most people, but not the Schofields. On the banks of Buffalo they raised four children: Amanda, Daniel, Emily, and Thomas. Remarkably, there was time left over for additional pursuits such as music. John and Diana have mastered numerous instruments. Both became leaders in local bluegrass bands, performing regularly. Was that enough to satisfy the creative power? No.

Diana was driven to write songs, plays, pageants, and poetry, while managing a home and a store and coaching her children's sports. In her spare time she has given music lessons to scores of students as well as to her own family.

The ancient Buffalo spirit directed John to his shop across the road. There he became an artisan, meticulously crafting fine musical instruments, mostly mandolins. They sold well. John designed and built power equipment that could speed the production line. He created and sold more than a gross of mandolins alone. Still the spirit called for more, and John responded.

This time it was not woodworking, but metal crafting. From bits and pieces of scrapped machinery John created an unbelievably intricate device that can be described as "art in motion." More than eight feet tall, the complicated contrivance makes multiple billiard balls dance and leap in accord with most of the known laws of physics, nonstop. The finished product weighs a half-ton and represents thousands of hours in construction. It has entertained throngs of viewers at various expositions, including the Virginia Museum of Science. The intriguing instrument has brought John some notoriety and may eventually offer him fame. All who watch it are impressed. One man was moved to comment, "The genius who designed this device should never have to work again."

Wealth and fame would never stop John. He loves to create. His active brain is hatching new projects every minute, whether at his day job or upon the side of his beloved mountain. When he wanted a chalet above the lake that he had created, John selected trees, fashioned them into various kinds of lumber, and built a striking cottage from materials at hand. Diana's cheerful energy is dependable, too, complementing and balancing their life together. The entire family is musically gifted. Together they join to offer their talents as an ensemble at Oxford Church on upper Buffalo.

The Schofields love what they do and intend to continue. When asked to name the crowning achievement of his fruitful life, John easily responded, "Being a parent to my children." When asked why he invents things, he says simply, "Because I have to."

Is there something in the waters of Buffalo or the air or the chemistry of the soil? What force attracted the Schofields to this particular location? How do we account for the historic procession of gifted residents? What is it that inspires and propels them to extraordinary achievement? Uncle Bob would no doubt tell us, if he were here today. I think he might call it the Spirit of Snakefoot. That spirit, whether natural or divine, may be what compels and controls John and Diana today, just as it has done for others in the past.

Go to Upper Buffalo. Spend some time. The spirit is still active. You may be surprised at what it does in your life.

Historic Homes
of the
Oxford Communitty

Historic Homes
of the
Oxford Communitty

"Magdalena," 60 Rose Farm Hill Lane

- Home of Rev. Dr. and Mrs. Horace Douty, situated on 9 acres of historic Thorn Hill, the western edge of Lexington, Virginia.

- Completed in 2007, estate named "Magdalena" for reasons given in this book.

- When another Presbyterian pastor, Alexander Craighead, owned this ridge in 1739, he called it "Mispeh" which in Hebrew translates to "Watchtower Hill."

Tardy-Leech Property, 2218 Spring Valley Road

- Property was owned c. 1838 by John Clarkson.
- After Clarkson's death, daughter Juliette Clarkson Dixon became owner.
- Sold to W.F. Johnston and W.B.F. Leech, who sold it to Robert B. Brubeck.
- In 1894, deeded to James R. Tardy.
- Home of James R. Replogle Tardy and Mary Elizabeth Montgomery Tardy family; home of Frank Lee Tardy and Bertie Montgomery Tardy.
- Home of Jennings Tardy and Marie Jarvis Tardy; childhood home of Richard Tardy, David Tardy, Jean Tardy Clark.
- Home of David Tardy and Phyllis Bennington Tardy. Current home of Charles B. Leech IV and Linda Craun Leech.

Tardy-Leech-Potter Property, 307 Oxford Lane

- Home of Kate Tardy, formerly owned by Frank Leech.
- Current home of Steve and Martha Potter; childhood home of Christopher Potter and Ross Potter.

Rader-Potter Property, 109 Churchview Lane

- Family home of George Rader, nephew John Ayres resided here for many years.
- Mrs. Cora Siron served as Mr. Rader's housekeeper after his wife's death.
- Current home of Charles A. Potter Jr. and Joan Gilliam Potter; childhood home of Marnie Potter Caldwell, Susanne Potter O'Neal, and Charles A. "Chas" Potter III.

Leech Property, 518 Bluegrass Trail

- Former home of J. Henry Leech and Nellie McMaster Leech family, childhood home of Dr. Frank McConnell Leech, William McMaster Leech, Elizabeth Leech Whitehurst and Gladys Leech Grant.

- Recent home of William McMaster "Bill" Leech Jr., and Ruth Wilson Morrison Leech; childhood home of Dalia "Day" Leech Ferguson, William McMaster "Will" Leech III, and Frank Leech.

- Note front of Oxford Church in left background.

Hall-Rader-Leech-Willa Property, 678 Blue Grass Trail

- Former home of Captain James Hall family, Harvey and John D. Rader families.
- Owned by Dr. Frank Leech.
- Home of Jack Kateley and Kathleen McKee Kateley.
- Home of Harriet England Rhodenizer and Henry Rhodenizer.
- Home of Frank A. Willa Sr. family. Current home of Doreen Willa.

"The Old Oxford Manse," 821 Bluegrass Trail

- Home for many pastors of Oxford Church.
- After Dr. George West Diehl and Mrs. Iva Diehl moved to "Dundee," house was used by other families, including William "Bill" Ayres and Coleen Saville Ayres.
- Current home of Robert E. "Moot" Rhodenizer and Robert E. "Bobby" Rhodenizer Jr.

Campbell-Morrison-Harris Property, 1110 Bluegrass Trail

- Former home of Granville Campbell, former home of Robert and Minnie Morrison; childhood home of R. Bruce Morrison, Gertrude Morrison, Julia Morrison Ferris, and Ralph Morrison.
- Current home of Will and Jane Harris; childhood home of Mary Elizabeth "Mary Beth" Harris, William Leslie "Lee" Harris, IV, Thomas Houston "Tommy" Harris and Anna Katherine Harris.

Saville-Harris Property, 56 South Buffalo Road

- Former home of J. Sidney Saville family; childhood home of Charles Sidney Saville, Kathleen Saville, Judith Saville, Elizabeth Saville, and William Gladstone Smith Saville.
- Home of Charles and Priscilla Saville, childhood home of Elizabeth Dodson Saville Fauber.
- Currently owned by Will and Jane Harris family.

"Belmont," 1240 Bluegrass Trail

- Families of "Belmont" include: Major Adolph Elhart (1896–1913); Lackey (1913–1946); Johenning (1947–1954); Frith (1954–1970); Fellner (1970–1986).
- Current home of Kermit and Marty Rockett.

"Ashland Farm," Leech-Swink-Glick Property, 2332 Bluegrass Trail

- Original property of John Steel Leech; childhood home of William Bolivar Finley (W.B.F.) Leech.
- Home of Daniel Swink and Jennie Caruthers Houston Swink; childhood home of John Milton Swink and Mattie Ella Swink McCorkle.
- Home of D. Lawrence Glick and Patsy Armentrout Glick; childhood home of Patricia Ann Glick Donald, David Glick, and Betty Lou Glick Jones.
- Current home of Patsy Glick and Patricia Glick Donald and Robert E. "Bob" Donald.

"Ingleside," Leech-Pyne-Leech Property, 32 Spring Branch Road

- Built by William Bolivar Finley (W.B.F.) Leech over a five-year period (1870–1875).
- Bricks for "Ingleside" were made using the same molds as used to build Oxford Church.
- Home left to W.B.F. Leech's only daughter, Ella Leech Pyne, and her husband, Ernest O. Pyne; Charles Bolivar Leech Jr. purchased the property from Ella's heirs in 1940.
- From 1950 to present, home of Charles Bolivar Leech III and Mackey Williams Leech; childhood home of Charles Bolivar Leech IV, Margaret "BeBe" Leech Showalter, and Sarah Leech Dudley.

Leech Property, 2479 Bluegrass Trail

- House built around 1870, home of Charles Bolivar Leech family.

- Originally located across North Buffalo Creek.

- Home of W.B.F. Leech's grandson, Bolivar Leech and Isabel Huffman Leech; home of Houston Leech and Ruby Bennington Leech; home of Leroy Leech; home of Charles B. Leech IV and Linda Leech.

- Current home of Charles B. Leech V and his sister, Jennifer Craun Leech.

**Hotinger-Hartbarger-Hall-Showalter-Mahood Property,
2104 Bluegrass Trail**

- Former home of John Norman Hotinger and Hattie Hotinger; childhood home of Ivy Hotinger Garing, Joseph Hotinger, Mayre Hotinger Rayder and Norman Hotinger.
- Briefly home of Waitman Deacon family; birthplace of W.R."Tink" Deacon.
- Owned by Ray W. Hotinger; owned by Howard Hartbarger.
- Home of Nelson Hall and Gatha Reynolds Hall; childhood home of Tonya Hall Fontenot and Norris Hall.
- Owned by Charlie Showalter.
- Currently owned by Tina and James Mahood Jr.

Johnston Property, 420 South Buffalo Road

- Property of William Finley Johnston. Home of James Granville Johnston and Lora Shafer Johnston; childhood home of John William Johnston and Mary Campbell Johnston Brady.
- Currently owned by John William Johnston.

Johnston-Huffman Property, 861 South Buffalo Road

- Home of Martha "Pat" Johnston Rodriques and Nathaniel V. Rodriques when Mr. Rodriques was principal of Palmer High School (1912–1920).
- Home of Grover and Nettie Huffman, and last home of Isabel Huffman Leech.
- Currently owned by E.G. Huffman family.

Johnston-Hickman-Herrington-Fleming Property, 34 Maggies Lane

- Former home of James Montgomery Johnston.
- Childhood home of Mrs. Maggie Hickman Herrington, Merset Hickman, James "Tip" Hickman, and Cecil Hickman.
- Longtime residence of Mrs. Herrington.
- Childhood home of W.R. "Tink" Deacon.
- Current home of Stock and Jean Fleming.

**"Dundee," Hamilton-Shafer-Diehl-Erchul Property,
1512 South Buffalo Road**

- Home believed to be built about 1781.
- Former home of Robert "Bob" Hamilton.
- Home of John A. Shafer family; childhood home of Iva Shafer Diehl, Lora Shafer Johnston, Lillian Shafer, and Dora Shafer Ackerley.
- Home of Dr. George West Diehl and Iva Shafer Diehl.
- Home of Charles Zink and Joanna Zink.
- Currently owned by Ronald A. Erchul.

Short-Dixon Property, 673 Kygers Hill Road

- Once owned by Henry Kiger Short and Ollie S. Kirkpatrick Short; childhood home of Louise Short Lomax.
- Home of Buford Dixon and Mabel Tolley Dixon; boyhood home of Thomas A. Dixon.
- Short Hill is named after the Short family.

"Short Hill Farm,"
Replogle-Tardy-Leech-Poore-Norwood-Harris Property,
187 Kygers Hill Road

- Original home of the Replogle family.
- Home of John Tardy.
- Property owned by Dr. Frank Leech; home for William Farrow family when he served as foreman for Leech Hereford Farms.
- Owned by Loye C. Poore family.
- Owned by Roger Norwood. Home of William L. "Bill" Harris Jr., and Louise Harris; childhood home of William L. "Will" Harris III.
- Current home of Louise Harris.

"Bellevue,"
Bell-Reeves-Clayton Property, 1166 Zollman's Mill Road

- Former home of William Bell and Sallie Bell; childhood home of Elizabeth Bell McClung and Margarite Bell Moore.
- Home of Colonel John H. "Jack" Reeves and Trudy Reeves; childhood home of Nell Reeves McDaniel, John Reeves Jr., Trudy Reeves Melvin, and Terry Reeves Whitmore.
- Currently owned by Sarah Clayton.

**"Stone House Farm," Davidson-Macdonald Property,
1036 Zollman's Mill Road**

- House originally built in 1775 by William Davidson.
- Numerous owners included Rev. Andrew B. Davidson, pastor of Oxford Church, and John A. Mateer.
- The Miller family resided here for many years.
- Current home of Bruce and Sonia "Sunny" Macdonald.

**"Boz Zollman's," Zollman-Irvine-Potter Property,
1146 Collierstown Road**

- Former home of Boz Zollman.
- Home of Bob Irvine family. Currently owned by the Charles Potter Jr. family.

"Grey Fox Farm," Mateer-Taylor Property, 283 Mateer Lane

- Home of John A. Mateer, childhood home of Louise Mateer Estes and Homer Mateer.
- Current home of Lee and Rebecca Taylor; childhood home of Rollin Taylor, Weston Taylor, Jessie Taylor, and Leila Taylor.

"Locust Hill," Donald Property, 602 Zollman's Mill Road

- Home of William M. "Bill" Donald and Margaret Garber Donald, childhood home of Mary Lincoln Donald Black, Frances Donald Claytor, Billy Donald, and Robert E. "Bob" Donald.

"The Bolivar House at Bolivar Mills," 1990 Collierstown Road

- Home for many families over the years.
- Home of Ira Dixon.
- Owned at one time by Robert and Edith M. Zollman.
- More recently, the home of Ruby Farrow.
- Current owners are William E. Files and Shirley Z. Files of Williamsburg, VA.

Clemmer-Leech Property, 394 Blue Grass Trail

- Former home of Phil Clemmer and Nica Montgomery Clemmer.

- Property owned by Dr. Frank Leech.

- Current home of William M. "Will" Leech and Sharon Rhodenizer Leech; childhood home of Holly Tucker Leech Clifton and William Jacob Leech.

McCorkle-Henderson Property, 866 Kygers Hill Road

- Former home of J. Gold and Mattie Ella Swink McCorkle; boyhood home of Stuart Alexander McCorkle, and Daniel Swink McCorkle.
- Current home of Hugh and Ann Henderson; childhood home of Charles Henderson, Elizabeth Henderson, Edward Henderson and John Henderson.
- Photo from about 1980.

"Oakdale," Deacon Property, 1900 Bluegrass Trail

- Oakdale Post Office and home of James D. Deacon family, including Mary Margaret Deacon, James Palmer Deacon, Anna Virginia Deacon Withrow, and Lolita Elizabeth Deacon Phillips.
- Photo from about 1900.

**"Spring Branch Farm," Wilson-Saville-Anderson Property,
504 Spring Branch Road**

- Captain James F. Wilson built house in 1834; home of Robert Saville and Jane Wilson Saville family; childhood home of Robert Lucian Saville, John W. Saville, Estie Saville, Minnie Saville Morrison, Harry Saville.
- Home of Estie Saville.
- Owned by Robert L. Saville.
- Owned by Florence Saville Anderson.
- Home of Herman and Cottie Hall Glenn; childhood home of Polly Glenn Dudley, Ruby Glenn Deacon Rohr, and Delbert Glenn.
- Home of Clinton and Kathleen Anderson.
- Current home of John Stuart Anderson.

"RoseBrooke Farm," John Saville-Vansant-Irwin-Schuster Property, 546 Spring Branch Road

- Former home of John W. Saville and Mary J.E. Miller Saville; childhood home of Harry Saville and Ida Saville Moore until the early death of their parents.
- Owned by Harry Lucian Saville and Cora Trekle Saville and later by their son, Robert Edwin Saville, who lived in Martinsville, VA.
- Home of Elmer and Kerry Vansant.
- Owned for a short time by Erlene Irwin.
- Currently owned by Steven B. Schuster and Cynthia L. Schuster.

**"Willow Manor," Saville-Anderson-Hotchkiss Property,
1150 Wide Gap Road**

- Robert Lucian Saville and Annie Hotinger Saville homeplace; childhood home of Herbert Saville and Ruth Saville (who died while attending Palmer High School); lifetime home of Florence Jane Saville Anderson and, later her husband, Nelson Stokes Anderson; childhood home of Clinton Lee Anderson.
- Current home of Pierson and Ellen Hotchkiss in Dry Hollow/ Wide Gap; childhood home of Pierson Hotchkiss III and Jackson Hotchkiss.

Clark-Scott-Smith Property, 229 Bull Run Lane

- Former home of James David Clark and Eliza Jane Potter Clark.
- Home of Lee K. Scott and Lily Worth Scott; childhood home of Margaret Scott Hust.
- Current home of W. Frank Smith and Juanita Hall Smith; childhood home of William Lacy "Billy" Smith, Jerry Wayne Smith, and Sandra Ann Smith Bryant.

Clark-Irvine Property, 591 Bull Run Lane

- Former home of Wilson Clark and Minnie Blanche Siron Clark; childhood home of Margaret Clifton Clark Newell, Eliza Jane Clark Goodbar, James Wilson Clark Jr., John Houston Clark, William Chester Clark, H. Custis Clark, Erma Elizabeth Clark Irvine, Virginia Coleman Clark Black, Beulah Mae Clark Brown, and Aubrey Carson Clark.

- Home of Pete Irvine and Erma Clark Irvine. Current home of Erma Irvine.

Ruff-Saville-Turpin Property, 21 Question Mark Lane

- House built by Frank J. Ruff. Harry R. Saville bought property in 1904; childhood home of Minnie Saville Turpin, Edna Saville White, Lelia Deacon Saville Hayslette, Reece Saville, and Lenna Lucille Saville Harris.

- Home of John T. "Jack" Turpin Sr. and Minnie Saville Turpin; childhood home of John T. Turpin Jr., Eugene Samuel Turpin, Nancy Josephine "Jo" Turpin Dunlap, Vinda Turpin Bryant, Mary Lee Turpin Wood and Thomas McClung "Tommy" Turpin.

- Current home of Karen Vanness Turpin, widow of Tommy Turpin, and her two sons, T.J. and John Turpin.

"Old Anderson Homeplace," 553 Murat Road

- Former home of John Replogal Anderson and Eliza Jane Palmer Anderson; childhood home of Robert Milton Anderson, Jacob Anderson, Sarah Jane Anderson Montgomery, Susan Ann Anderson Lam, Horatio Thompson Anderson, and James McElwee Anderson.

- Home of James McElwee Anderson and Mattie Hutton Anderson; childhood home of Robert Teague Anderson, Ethel Gilmore Anderson, John Kyle Anderson, Gard Hutton Anderson, Harry Palmer "Hal" Anderson, Nelson Stokes Anderson, Estelle Vernon Anderson, and Aline Baker Anderson.

- Home of Milton Dunlap Anderson and Mary Moore McCorkle Anderson; childhood home of Martha McCorkle Anderson Hust and Carol Anderson Rose.

"Old Kirk Place," Kirkpatrick-Montgomery Property, 853 Murat Road

- Thomas M. Kirkpatrick and Eliza Taylor Kirkpatrick, deeded 107 acres to son John F. Kirkpatrick in 1884.
- Present house built in the late 1880s.
- Home of John F. Kirkpatrick and Fannie E. Firebaugh Kirkpatrick; childhood home of Daisy E. Kirkpatrick Montgomery and Ollie S. Kirkpatrick Short.
- Daisy Kirkpatrick and Graham Montgomery married at the house March 6, 1905, by Rev. J.P. Smith Jr., pastor of Oxford Church.
- Property deeded to Daisy K Montgomery in 1912 by John F. Kirkpatrick and Fannie F. Kirkpatrick.
- Upon Daisy's death in 1923, property passed to her three children: Henry Kirkpatrick Montgomery, Ellen F. Montgomery, and Everett Graham "Bill" Montgomery.

Continued on next page

Continued from previous page

- Home of Henry K. Montgomery and Bertha Peplinski Montgomery until 1940; childhood home of Milton G Montgomery.

- House leased from 1940 to 1954, to renters Ted and Virginia Sorrells and then W.S. "Dub" Johnson and Helen Deacon Johnson.

- Milton G. Montgomery and Shirley Louise Swink began married life here, buying the property in 1958; childhood home of Emily Montgomery Conroy and Beverly Montgomery Nedrow.

- Current home of Shirley Montgomery and her brother, Robert H. "Bobby" Swink.

McCown-Tardy Property, 1978 Spring Valley Road

- Former home of Walter McCown and Margaret Tardy McCown; childhood home of James Samuel McCown, William Albert McCown, and Albert T. McCown.
- Home of Jennings J. Tardy on three different occasions.
- Current home of Amanda Tardy Conway and family.

Fix Property, 73 Mallard Duck Lane

- Former home of Freeman Fix and Bessie Smith Fix.
- Home of Preston Alexander Fix and Elizabeth Taylor Fix; childhood home of Fred Fix, Nancy Fix Rogers, Donna Fix Tyree, and Phil Taylor Fix.
- Current home of Phil Fix family.

Barger-Dixon Property, 1002 Spring Valley Road

- Former home of Woodrow Barger. Home of Thomas A."Tom" Dixon and Betty Swink Dixon; childhood home of Teresa Dixon Irvine, Tamara Dixon Thompson, and Sue Dixon Woodruff.
- Current home of Betty Dixon and her mother, Marie Zollman Swink.

Wilson-Rhodenizer Property, 504 South Buffalo Road

- Former home of Walter Wilson.
- Home of Harry F. Rhodenizer and Helen Potter Rhodenizer; childhood home of David Samuel Rhodenizer, Henry Luther Rhodenizer. Sandra Rhodenizer Thompson, and Sara Frances Rhodenizer Meradith.
- Current home of Helen Rhodenizer.

**"The Lam Place," Lam-Diehl-Erchul Property,
1368 South Buffalo Road**

- Former home of Andrew Calvin Lam and Susan Ann Anderson Lam; childhood home of William Irby Lam, Robert Harry Lam, Dalia Anderson Lam Ruff, James Finley Lam, Claude White Lam, and Mamie Palmer Lam Morrison.
- Current home of Ronald A. Erchul and Beverly Erchul.

Swink-Clemmer Property, 44 Swink Lane

- Built by Milton Swink in 1898; home of John Milton Swink and Mary Montgomery Swink.
- Current home of Kathryn Weeks Clemmer.

**"Hull Morrison's," Morrison-Elliott-Elmes Property,
20 Swink Lane**

- Former home of J. Hull Morrison and Mamie Lam Morrison; childhood home of John Hull Morrison, Marian Morrison Lutz, Dorothy Morrison Schoenhut, Ruth Wilson Morrison Leech.
- Home of Brenda Elliott. Current home of Ann Elmes.

**"Clyde Morrison's," Morrison-Crawshaw Property,
10 Swink Lane**

- Former home of Clyde Wilson Morrison and Lillian Hotinger Morrison; childhood home of Jean Hotinger Morrison Barnes, Margaret Vivian Morrison Jarvis, and Carolyn Virginia Morrison Elliott.
- After Clyde Morrison's death, home of Lillian Hotinger Potter and Ray Potter Sr.
- Currently owned by Robert "Bob" Crawshaw and Lynn Crawshaw, who also live in Salem, VA.

"Hogue Place," Hogue-Yawars Property, 1822 Bluegrass Trail

- Former home of Harry Hogue and Hattie Cummings Hogue; childhood home of James Hogue, Dora Hogue DeVuono, Ruby Hogue Deacon, Harry Hogue Jr., and Hilda Hogue.
- Currently owned by Dave and Carolyn Yawars.

Hotinger-Green-Knick Property, 173 Moores Creek Road

- Former home of Lewis "Lou" L. Hotinger and Hattie Hotinger; childhood home of Helen Hotinger Nuckols, Basil Hotinger, Gertude Hotinger, Jane Hotinger Showalter, John T. Hotinger Fulmider, Mary M. Hotinger Ashby, Reva Sieg Hotinger Haney, Sam Hotinger, and Willanna "Pick" Hotinger Peery.
- Home of Samuel and Mary Knick Green.
- Home of Fremont and Bessie Scott Knick.
- Current home of William Fremont "Bill" Knick III, and Jade Knick; childhood home of William Fremont "Will" Knick IV, and Harper Renee Knick.

"Black Homeplace," Black Property, 226 Moores Creek Road

- Former home of James Black and Susan Swink Black; childhood home of Mary Annie Black Beard, Clara Pearl Black Quinlan, Virginia Sadie Black, Peggy Black Cole, Alvah Nelson Black, James Howe Black and Madison Black.

- Home of Alvah Black and Mary Goodbar Black; childhood home of Frances Black Wheeler, Robert Beyers "Bobby" Black, James "Jim" Black, H. Arnold "Tootle" Black and Carol Elizabeth Black Hines.

- Current home of Richard Black family.

**"Paradox Farm," J. Edward Reid-Wapner Property,
118 Moores Creek Road**

- Former home of J. Edward Reid and Elsie Hogue Reid, former residence of J.D. Clemmer family and Eddie Reid.
- Currently owned by Mitch Wapner and Cynthia M. Downes.
- Current home of Brooks Channing.

"Joe Reid Place," Reid-Hall Property, 1551 South Buffalo Road

- House built by William Joseph "Joe" Reid.
- Home of William Joseph "Joe" Reid and Emma Frances Holt Reid; childhood home of James Edward Reid, Mary A. Elizabeth Reid, Dorthy Roberta Reid, Ida Mae Reid, Alleyne Georgia Reid, Helen Grace Virginia Reid, and Mattie Ella Lee Reid.
- Home of Mattie Reid Ackerly and children (twins Pauline Ackerly Morris Vanness and Christine Ackerly Frazier, and Jean Phyllis Ackerly Kellum) from 1933–1943 after death of her husband.
- Home of Helen Reid McDaniel and children (Geneva McDaniel Murray, Wendell McDaniel and Betsy Ann McDaniel) from 1940–1945, after death of her husband.
- Home of Ira and Christine Frazier and son Barney Allen Frazier from 1945 until 1953.

Continued on next page

Continued from previous page

- Home of James Coleman Hall and Ida Reid Hall; childhood home of Ida Marie Hall Paxton and Mary Frances Hall Rhodenizer.
- Eddie Reid was resident for several years.
- Home of James Edward Hall Sr. and Thelma Frazier Hall beginning 1961; childhood home of James Edward Hall Jr., Wanda Belinda Hall McDaniel, and Tammy Madge Hall Tew.
- Current home of Thelma Hall and her brother, John Wayne Frazier.

"Sideway" and "The Jake Saville Place,"
Saville-Richards Property, 2105 South Buffalo Road

- Former home of Jacob O. Saville and Maggie Saville; childhood home of Coleen Saville Ayres, Lodell Saville Allen, Della Saville Swink, Evade Betty Saville Miller, Bernice Margaret "Billie" Saville Black, Nancy Saville Wilkerson, Birdie Saville Mills, and Alice Jane Saville Greever.
- Current home of Steve and Wendy Richards.

Harry Reid-Schofield Property, 1437 Spring Branch Road

- Former home of Harry Reid, childhood home of Robert Reid, E. Malcolm "Mac" Reid, Fred Reid, Harry "Elwood" Reid, Edith Mae Reid Booth, and Douglas Reid.
- Current home of John Schofield and Diana Madsen Schofield, childhood of Amanda Schofield, Daniel Schofield, Emily Schofield, and Thomas Schofield.

"The Daniel Farm," 3105 South Buffalo Road

- Property is one of oldest in South Buffalo area, believed to be approximately 200 years old.
- Formerly owned by John T. Manspile.
- Purchased by Raymond R Daniel in 1917.
- Home of Raymond R. Daniel and wife Helen C. Daniel.
- After Raymond's death (1954), Helen continued to live in the house into the 1970s, until she was 91 years old.

Turpin-Clemmer-Leech Property, 861 South Buffalo Road

- Former home of Sam Turpin and Nan Reid Turpin.
- Home of Emmett Clemmer and Mary Thomas Clemmer.
- Current home of Larry Leech and Holly Clark Leech; childhood home of Blake Leech and Hank Leech.

**"Rapp Homeplace," Rapp-Parsons Property,
3293 South Buffalo Road**

- Former home of Mathias Rapp and Mary Saville Rapp, childhood home of James Sidney Parsons and William Wade "Billie" Parsons. Longtime residence of Bill and Coleen Ayres.

- Current home of Dr. James Parsons and his wife, Eleanor Parsons, and their children, Ruth Parsons and John Parsons.

Goodwin-Pursley Property, 3392 South Buffalo Road

- Former home of George and Sue Goodwin.
- Home of Lucy Pursley.
- Home of Ralph W. Pursley and Elsie Manspile Pursley; childhood home of Randall Pursley.

"Henderson Place," Henderson-Reid Property, 159 Saville Lane

- Former home of the Henderson family.
- Home of Charles Reid and Winnie Daniel Reid.
- Home of Daniel Reid and Mary Vassar Reid, childhood home of Benny Reid and Patsy Reid Landes. Pattie Reid Campbell and her husband, Greg Campbell, are current residents.

"Nicely Homeplace," Nicely Property, 1154 Little Dry Hollow Road

- Joseph "Joe" Nicely family home, home of Guy Nicely Sr. family, childhood home of Guy C. Nicely Jr., Dorothy Nicely McKenna, Louise Nicely Markham, Ruth Nicely Bullock, Paul Nicely, Kenton Lee Nicely, and Ovie Ellis Nicely.
- Current home of Paul W. "Buddy" Nicely Jr. family.

About the Author

Horace Dale Douty

Horace Dale Douty was born in Rockbridge but has lived most of his adult life in other places. A graduate of Washington and Lee University, Rev. Douty earned his advanced degrees from Union Theological Seminary in Virginia. He also graduated from the clinical School of Pastoral Care at Wake Forest University.

Over the last 50 years, Rev. Douty has served Presbyterian churches in North Carolina and Virginia. He and his wife Ellen moved to Rockbridge in 2004, and he became interim pastor for historic Oxford Presbyterian Church near Lexington the following year. That church congregation's unwavering interest in the stories of Oxford prompted the writing of this book. Rev. Douty remains as Oxford's pastor and continues to offer the congregation a new history lesson as part of each week's Sunday service.

The Doutys' home stands next door to the Thorn Hill Estate built in the 1780s by John and Magdalena Bowyer, both of whom are mentioned in this book and figured prominently in the earliest settlement of Borden's Grant and the founding of Lexington. Since no one knows the final resting place of the beautiful Magdalena, the Doutys gave their hilltop estate her name in an effort to perpetuate her memory. It was his research into Magdalena's life that first ignited Rev. Douty's curiosity about the area's history and began his Oxford writings.

www.ingramcontent.com/pod-product-compliance
Lightning Source LLC
Chambersburg PA
CBHW030409100426
42812CB00028B/2892/J